SAGE was founded in 1965 by Sara Miller McCune to support the dissemination of usable knowledge by publishing innovative and high-quality research and teaching content. Today, we publish over 900 journals, including those of more than 400 learned societies, more than 800 new books per year, and a growing range of library products including archives, data, case studies, reports, and video. SAGE remains majority-owned by our founder, and after Sara's lifetime will become owned by a charitable trust that secures our continued independence.

Los Angeles | London | New Delhi | Singapore | Washington DC | Melbourne

SAGE was founded in 1965 by Sara Miller McCune to support the dissemination of usable knowledge by publishing innovative and high-quality research and teaching content. Today, we publish over 900 journals, including those of more than 400 learned societies, more than 800 new books per year, and a growing range of library products including archives, data, case studies, reports, and video. SAGE remains majority-owned by our founder, and after Sara's lifetime will become owned by a charitable trust that secures our continued independence.

Los Angeles | London | New Delhi | Singapore | Washington DC | Melbourne

An Introduction to Political Theory

An Introduction to Political Theory

Amal Kumar Mukhopadhyay

Retired Principal and Professor of Political Science, Presidency College (Now Presidency University), Kolkata

SAGE | TEXTS

Los Angeles | London | New Delhi
Singapore | Washington DC | Melbourne

First published in 2019 by

SAGE | TEXTS

SAGE Publications India Pvt Ltd
B1/I-1 Mohan Cooperative Industrial Area
Mathura Road, New Delhi 110 044, India
www.sagepub.in

SAGE Publications Inc
2455 Teller Road
Thousand Oaks, California 91320, USA

SAGE Publications Ltd
1 Oliver's Yard, 55 City Road
London EC1Y 1SP, United Kingdom

SAGE Publications Asia-Pacific Pte Ltd
18 Cross Street #10-10/11/12
China Square Central
Singapore 048423

Published by Vivek Mehra for SAGE Publications India Pvt Ltd, typeset in 10.5/12.5 pt Adobe Garamond Pro by Zaza Eunice, Hosur, Tamil Nadu, India.

Library of Congress Cataloging-in-Publication Data

Names: Mukhopadhyay, Amal Kumar, author.
Title: An introduction to political theory/Amal Kumar Mukhopadhyay.
Description: New Delhi, India; Thousand Oaks, California: SAGE Publications, 2019. | Includes index.
Identifiers: LCCN 2018060837 | ISBN 9789353283018 (pbk.)
Subjects: LCSH: Political science. | Political science—India. | World politics. | India—Politics and government.
Classification: LCC JA71.M863 2019 | DDC 320.01—dc23 LC record available at https://lccn.loc.gov/2018060837

ISBN: 978-93-532-8301-8 (PB)

SAGE Team: Amit Kumar, Indrani Dutta, Sambhavi Shah, Arshita Saxena and Kanika Mathur

To Rupa
with love and affection

Contents

Preface xiii
About the Author xv

Chapter 1
The Meaning of Politics 1

Chapter 2
The Society 8

Chapter 3
The State 15

Chapter 4
The Civil Society 28

Chapter 5
Power 36

Chapter 6
Freedom 46

Chapter 7
Equality 55

Chapter 8
Rights 63

Chapter 9
Justice 71

Chapter 10
Law 80

Chapter 11
Citizenship 86

Chapter 12
Political Culture 93

CHAPTER 13
Democracy 102

CHAPTER 14
Political Ideology 112

CHAPTER 15
Government 138

CHAPTER 16
Social and Political Changes 156

CHAPTER 17
Crisis of Indian Political Theory 163

Index I–1

Detailed Contents

Preface xiii
About the Author xv

Chapter 1
The Meaning of Politics **1**
Introduction 1
Of Political Science, Theory and Thought 3
Study of Politics 5

Chapter 2
The Society **8**
Introduction 8
Evolution of Society 10
State and Society 11

Chapter 3
The State **15**
Introduction 15
The Idea of State and Related Riddles 18
State, Sovereignty and Government 20
Obedience to State 22
Concluding Observations 25

Chapter 4
The Civil Society **28**
Introduction 28
Nature of Civil Society 30
Civil Society and India 32
Civil Society and Democracy 33

Chapter 5
Power **36**
Introduction 36
Power and Politics 39
Power and Compliance 40
Source of Power 41
Power and Authority 43

CHAPTER 6
Freedom **46**
Introduction 46
Evolution of the Concept of Freedom 48
Political Freedom 50
Individual Freedom 51
Possibility of Freedom 53

CHAPTER 7
Equality **55**
Introduction 55
Types of Equality 57
Social Equality 59
Social Equality: The Case of India 59

CHAPTER 8
Rights **63**
Introduction 63
Source of Rights 64
Meaningful Use of Rights 66
Human Rights 67

CHAPTER 9
Justice **71**
Introduction 71
Pre-Renaissance Conceptualization of Social Justice 72
Renaissance and After: The Concept of Social Justice 74
Rawls' Theory of Justice 75
A Note on the Nature of Justice 78
Concluding Observations 79

CHAPTER 10
Law **80**
Introduction 80
The State and Its Law 83
Nature of Law 84

CHAPTER 11
Citizenship **86**
Introduction 86
Characteristics of a Citizen 88
Duties and Rights of a Citizen 89
Citizenship: New Dimensions 91

CHAPTER 12
Political Culture **93**
Introduction 93
Origin of a Political Culture 95
Evolution of Political Culture 97
Political Culture and Political System 99

CHAPTER 13
Democracy **102**
Introduction 102
As a Form of Government 103
Democracy and the Third World 105
Forms of Democracy 107
Critiques of Democracy 110

CHAPTER 14
Political Ideology **112**
Introduction 112
Liberalism 113
Anarchism 118
Marxism 122
Fascism 127
Gandhism 131

CHAPTER 15
Government **138**
Introduction 138
The Legislature 139
The Executive 144
Bureaucracy 148
The Judiciary 150

CHAPTER 16
Social and Political Changes **156**
Introduction 156
Importance of Change 157
Mode of Change 159

CHAPTER 17
Crisis of Indian Political Theory **163**
Introduction 163
Post-Independence Situation 165

Index I–1

Preface

This book, a product of many decades' experience of teaching political theory at Presidency College, Kolkata, is meant to give a precise, analytical and critical account of the basics of political theory without unnecessary fabrication. It focuses on all the concepts generally in use in political theory so that it becomes a comprehensive one. As readers will note, at various instances the book provides a glimpse of its originality by subjecting to criticism a few of the standard notions presented by modern renowned political scientists and frequently cites Indian examples which are rarely found in books, both Western and Indian, on political theory. On that score, I think, the book may claim novelty.

It took me a year to complete writing this book. As I write this preface, I fondly recall that a part of it was written in the guest room of Rashtrapati Bhavan, where I stayed for some time as a special guest of the then honourable President of India and my life-long dearest friend, Sri Pranab Mukherjee. I am thankful to his staff who provided me with the writing material and made my stay comfortable.

I shall be very happy if the book serves the need of the students of political science at the graduate level and inspires them to think anew about political theory.

Finally, I thank SAGE, New Delhi, for their interest and cooperation in publishing the book. I owe a special word of thanks to Ms Indrani Dutta, currently based at SAGE's Kolkata office, who took the trouble to travel in order to maintain liaison between SAGE and me over the last few months.

ABOUT THE AUTHOR

A noted political scientist and a constitutional expert, Professor Amal Kumar Mukhopadhyay is a product of Presidency College (now Presidency University), Kolkata, and the London School of Economics and Political Science, London. Professor Mukhopadhyay spent his entire professional career at Presidency College, first as a senior professor and then as the Head of the Department of Political Science. He retired in the year 1997 as the principal of Presidency College and since then has closely been involved in teaching and writing on subjects of his interest.

Some of his well-known publications include *The Ethics of Obedience* (1967), *Society and Politics in Contemporary India* (edited, 1974), *Political Sociology* (1977), *The Bengali Intellectual Tradition* (edited, 1979), *The Political Miscellany* (edited, 1986), *Western Political Thought: From Plato to Marx* (1988), *A Journey across the Indian Constitution* (2017) and *Metaphysics, Morals and Politics: An Enquiry into the Ideas of T.H. Green* (2017).

1
CHAPTER

The Meaning of Politics

INTRODUCTION

Notes

We frequently use the term 'politics' without exactly knowing what it means and what it is all about. Politics, of course, is an activity. But on the nature of this activity, theoreticians so far have offered varied opinion. Thus, traditionalists have viewed politics as an activity centring round political power holders and political power seekers. However, as political power is mostly a monopoly of the State, it virtually amounts to saying that politics is what is functional in the arena of the State and its organs, and not in the society. This, no doubt, is a very narrow definition of politics. Yet it reigned for hundreds of years until the 20th century.

With the onset of the 20th century, there began a persistent attempt to liberate politics from the confines of the State and locate it in the wider area of society. In this matter, Arthur Bentley and Graham Wallas were the pioneers. The former linked politics with the activities of social groups and the latter, viewing politics from the angle of empirical psychology, interpreted politics in terms of human behaviour. Much later, Charles Merriam of Chicago University underscored political behaviour as the content of politics. Very soon, Merriam transfused his ideas into a group of his students in Chicago University, each of whom later became an important political scientist and fully subscribed to the views of their teacher. This way, political behaviouralism began dominating the realm of political science for at least two decades. True, behaviouralism provided a new

Notes

definition of politics completely different from the traditional view, but its lacuna lays in its emphasis that behaviour is the only stuff of politics. Indeed behaviour may be a motivator behind politics as an activity, but in actual practice politics involves many other components such as latent longing for power, a desire to exercise power in a way salutary to one's benefit and many other things which cannot be manifested in external behaviour. Besides, there is a logical fallacy, for what motivates an activity cannot be regarded as the same as that activity. No wonder the euphoria about behavioural politics eventually subsided.

Meanwhile, David Easton, in order to give a sound farewell to the State and give social dimension to politics published his *The Political System* in 1953. In this book, he defined politics as 'the authoritative allocation of values in a society'. By this definition, he ably discarded the traditional notion of State-oriented politics and established politics clearly as a social activity. This definition establishes the thesis that politics is workable even in the absence of the State and, hence it is essentially a social activity. But to the question that who makes this authoritative allocation, Easton has no clear answer. In fact, Easton's definition suffers from some kind of automatism, that is, he takes it for granted that authoritative allocation operates automatically. But one cannot disregard the fact that the term 'authoritative' implies an imposing entity which has enough power to force everyone to accept allocation without question, and this could be nothing else than the State armed with extreme coercive power. Thus, although Easton avows himself to be a theorist to have been able to sweep away the concept of the State, but through his definition the State very much creeps in.

In the early 1960s, some theorists appeared on the scene to set up a new definition of politics that fits in well with the idea of politics as a social activity. They argued that whenever in a society there is any conflict or disagreement and someone resolves this conflict or disagreement, there is politics. This definition undoubtedly adds fullest social dimension to politics; that is, politics is admittedly proved to be a social activity. However, the overenthusiasm of these theorists to put politics in a social frame led them to argue that when two babies quarrel over the possession of a toy and further when their mother eventually appears to settle this conflict among her babies, the entire scenario reveals the working of politics. But this is really an absurd proposition, for these babies quarrel rather instinctively as devoid of any power of judgement they just love to have the toy, and emotionally attached to their mother they accept what is settled by her. Thus, it is too much to say that these babies and their mother are engaged in politics. Further, assuming that the existence and working of the State can in no way be ignored in actual practice—and this by any measure is not a false assumption—it is difficult to accept that every policy taken at the level of the State is an outcome of any conflict or disagreement. Hence, to understand the true meaning of politics what is required is to formulate a definition that suits well both the State and the society.

Notes

This is possible only when we agree to accept that any decision and its proper implementation constitute the core of politics. If politics is defined in this way, it can be equally applicable both to the State and to the society. Thus, a decision and its implementation by any organ of the State may be said to be an example of politics. On the other hand, a decision and its implementation by a social organization and even inside a family would be taken as involving politics. Again, this kind of definition would help us avoid the one-sided view of politics, for it would establish that politics applies not exclusively to the State or to the society, but it is both social and political.

But it would be a sheer hyperbole to say that any kind of decision breeds politics. Indeed, a decision to result in politics must satisfy certain conditions. First, it must be preceded by a rational choice. Second, this rational choice must be coupled with astute judgement. Third, it must be ensured that execution of this decision does not unnecessarily harm anyone. Thus, when someone in a fit of excitement suddenly attacks somebody else or when a person commits a murder, it is no politics. In the first case, there is a decision, but it does not follow from rational choice and judgement, whereas in the latter there may be a rational choice and judgement, but execution of the decision is extremely harmful. Similarly, conflict between two persons may be politics if it is proved that this conflict is the result of judgement taken by both and, further, if this judgement is backed up by a rational choice.

OF POLITICAL SCIENCE, THEORY AND THOUGHT

Everywhere in the world today, the study of politics goes by the name of political science. There are, however, some exceptions. For instance, in London School of Economics the department of political science is still known as the Department of Politics and Government. Originally, political science was called political economy. However, after the academics of the USA had invented the epithet 'political science', the world gradually accepted it. But controversy on the use of this expression still persists. Hence, it is necessary to settle the question whether political science can be truly called a science.

In the post-Second World War period, American theoreticians desperately tried to prove political science as a true science. Their main argument was that politics is an activity that is subject to quantification and measurement and, in order to prove it, they initiated newer methods and approaches. These methods and approaches have, of course, given a new look to the study of politics and extended its scope. But they have failed to prove that political science is as much a science as any other sciences. The reason is obvious. First, a political scientist may claim that all the raw materials he deals with are quantifiable and

Notes

measurable. But this may be true in some cases and not all. For instance, when a law is made by the legislature, which is a universal reality, no criterion is available to measure it. Further, if politics is considered as decision-making and its implementation then of the two at least decision-making is subjective in nature, which is not amenable to objective test. Second, a scientist invariably makes rigorous experiment with the variables he deals with. But since politics is a human activity, it cannot be subjected to experiment. Third, a scientist by his work arrives at truth which is universally applicable and mostly unchangeable. But a political scientist cannot claim that the truth he establishes applies at all times and in all the systems marked by a variety of conditions and political climate. Hence, political science is a misnomer or a science by default.

Political theory is one of the important branches of the study of politics. There have so far been many exponents of political theory. But none has ever tried to clarify what is meant by political theory. Hence, there is the need to define it. Actually, it is a conglomerate of generalized concepts related to politics and developed with the hope that these ideas would always be applicable, irrespective of time and space. But this high hope has often been belied because it is found that a theory developed by someone has in later times been replaced by another theorist with a newer theory. For instance, the theory of the State built up by Aristotle in the early Greek period has many times been amended by others' theory of the State, and this process still continues. This continuous change in political theory is due to the reason that every theorist has developed a theory in the context of his time and circumstances. Even Karl Marx in his theory could not foresee the conditions people are now facing in the 21st century. However, it has a brighter side in that this continuous flux has made political theory a dynamic discipline.

Like political theory, history of political thought is also taught as a branch of political science in almost all the universities of the world, including India. As these two subjects are often found to be almost similar to each other, those studying them sometimes seek for clarification as regards the difference between the two. This necessitates a clarification about the relation between the two. Masters of political thought in different ages by their creative genius produced various ideas mostly in response to the problems of their time. But they never intended to give these ideas a generalized form, that is, they never hoped that the ideas they advocated would go beyond the boundary of their time and prevailing conditions. In other words, they never meant their ideas to be universally applicable. Political theory, on the other hand, no doubt, equally deals with ideas or concepts. But there is always a conscious effort on the part of an exponent of political theory to give the idea he propounds a generalized form so that it may be universally applicable. Thus, the basic difference between political theory and political thought is that while the former is cast in generalization, the latter is devoid of it. Yet political theory is largely indebted to political thought, for political theory derives many of its sources from political thought. For instance, Plato's philosophy of distinguishing particular from the general idea and his conclusion that reality lies only in the general idea has inspired political theorists of all times to focus on generalization as the goal of their theories. Locke's ideas serve as the mainstay of the political theory of liberalism. Rousseau's thought is the root of the political theory of popular sovereignty and so on. Thus, it may be said that political thought and political theory are Siamese twins.

STUDY OF POLITICS

What is the foundation of the study of politics or, for that matter, what should be the correct approach to the study of politics? Earlier, political scientists were least concerned with the question, precisely until the beginning of the Second World War. But in the post-war period, the political scientists, particularly the American political scientists, took the approach to the study of politics as one of their main concerns.

For hundreds of years in the past, philosophy was treated as the keystone of political theory; that is, following Aristotle, many political theorists such as Bodin, Kant, Hegel and T. H. Green embraced philosophical approach to politics. Thus reigned the philosophical approach in the study of politics for long. But in the post-Second World War era, the American political scientists became very much vocal in contesting the validity of philosophical approach. Eventually, they abjured the philosophical approach and replaced it by the empirical approach. The point in favour of their move was that as politics is an activity subject to quantification and measurement, it has to be explained and understood only empirically and not through philosophy which is out and out rooted in abstraction. Another argument was that all political philosophers in the past developed their theories with the State as the centre of attraction. But politics cannot be accepted as a State-oriented activity, it is decidedly social.

As noted earlier, Charles Merriam and his Chicago School initiated this empirical approach by postulating political behaviour as the bedrock of politics. Later, David Easton introduced the systems analysis of politics. Then came in quick succession the communications approach, the structural–functional approach and so on. The advocates of these approaches were all agreed that politics operates in the larger sphere of a society and that it is to be explained and evaluated by an empirical standard. The ballyhoo raised by the empiricists immediately shook the academic circle. Many of the political scientists, particularly those of the Third World including India, hailed the empirical approach to politics as a symbol of modernism in political science. But this enthusiasm did not last long. Within a couple of decades, the empirical approach had to roll back and today in the 21st century one notices a rehabilitation of philosophy in political science. This predicament was inevitable, for, as noted earlier, politics is a human activity. Although this activity may be subject to external material factors, the origin of this activity is the mind of man which is so subjective and complex that it is impossible to put it to an objective and empirical test.

Philosophy is a study of man and the world. Obviously it is a holistic study in that it views man and the realities around him in a chain of totality. One of the main concerns of philosophy is to comprehend how mind reacts to reality and knows it. This is where the focus of philosophy is on mind and thus all human activities, including political activity following from the working of mind, come within the province of philosophy. It is true that mind is subjective and, therefore, it may be argued that what studies and analyses this subjective entity is destined to be abstract. This argument of course applies to the idealist philosophical tradition. But there is another kind of philosophy which is by no means steeped in abstraction. This is the empiricist philosophy, pioneered by the 17th-century English philosopher John Locke and serving as the veritable source of inspiration to the political scientists highlighting the importance of the empirical approach to politics. But, unlike these political scientists, the empiricist philosophy never said that realities known are quantifiable and measurable. It only said that reality is no fiction but fact, and that it may be known by the mind only when sensations through sense organs flow to the mind. Had the advocates of the empirical approach would have stopped at this point and tried to show that politics is not vague and abstract, but concrete reality subject to man's sense perception, then they could have been on the right track. But they took their empiricism too far and thus landed in trouble.

Again, the empirical approach to politics finally ended in focusing that political science is value-free. It was also claimed by the exponents of the empirical approach that by establishing the study of politics as value-free, they had been able to bring political science much closer to general science. But the assumption it involves is that a scientist is always engaged in value-free activity which is far from true. True, the scientist enquires into matter and motion, and makes his experiment with material tools. But behind his activity, he has a purpose which is to do good to mankind. Thus, he is much conscious of what is morally good and what is morally bad, and opts for the former, avoiding the latter. This shows that a scientist, while beginning with a hypothesis that he subjects to experiment, first makes a value judgement. It may be counterclaimed that when he invents destructive arms such as nuclear weapon doing great harm to mankind, he is denuded of all values. But one has to remember that he does it not on his own but only at the behest of the power-hungry State he serves. Thus, when the scientist is able to make fission and fusion of atoms, he has in his mind only the objective that this would lead to the generation of nuclear energy that would supplement the traditional sources of energy and thus help the world. But when he makes out of it a nuclear weapon, he actually is forced to do it by the political masters keen on being a superpower in the world. Thus, science by any measure is not value-free. The only tragedy is that some modern political scientists insistent on the validity of their empirical approach refuse to accept it.

Notes

Further, in the empirical approach, politics is treated as a phenomenon which is observed or is observable. Hence, the argument continues—politics is not normative. That is, the task of the political scientist is to take an empirical view of what is happening and not to prescribe what should happen. But a political scientist is after all a social and political animal having the responsibility to make a better society and politics. In other words, he is not a photographer but an artist trying to recreate politics with his imagination and sense of values. Viewed from this angle also, political science is not value-free. And that proves that no empirical approach to politics can ever replace the philosophical approach having the longest tradition in the study of politics.

2 CHAPTER

The Society

Notes

INTRODUCTION

In Chapter 1, we have seen that politics is a kind of activity which operates both in the society and the State. This naturally evokes the question: What is meant by society and the State? In this chapter, we shall concentrate on the meaning of society, and that of the State will be looked into in Chapter 3.

When Greek philosopher Aristotle, by implication, described man as a social animal, it seemed to be a very innovative account. But today if we use it, it will just sound a cliché, for a man living in abstraction from society is now so absurd a proposition that to call man a social animal amounts only to tautology. However, this was not so in primitive times. Man then, an erratic wanderer in jungles with little needs to meet and with his undeveloped mind, could live alone without caring for the company or cooperation of others. But as man's mind began to reach a developed stage and as, accordingly, rose the quantum of his needs, he realized that he could no longer afford to be self-dependent, but very much required the assistance and association of others. He now found that he could not collect the kind of things such as food, shelter and clothes he badly needed for living by his lone efforts. Hence, he turned to others and voluntarily joined them to meet his growing needs. This is how society in a rudimentary form came into existence.

However, it was not a society in the truest sense. It was, at best, an associative or community living. Rooted in material needs, it only brought people together

Notes

to fight unitedly against adverse conditions for the purpose of satisfying their basic needs. This historical account may prompt one to draw the conclusion that material needs alone serve as the basis of society. But the subsequent historical developments point to the untenability of this conclusion, for while continuing with associative living, man eventually found that the area of his needs had so much expanded that he now needed cooperation and assistance from a larger number of people. He also discovered that he was an entity with many feelings such as pleasure, hopes and fear, which he must share with others, for otherwise they would quickly fade out, and as these feelings were a mirror of his own identity, unless shared with others, it might lead to a loss of his own identity. Further, the burden of his mental sufferings would be too heavy for him without having others to share it. For his physical sufferings too, he needed the help and assistance of others. Above all, he felt the necessity of just friendship and neighbourliness for his own mental recreation and peace. Thus, man decided to come closer to his fellow mates not alone for the fulfilment of his material needs but also for the satisfaction of his subjective self. This is how the associative living reached a higher phase now, where man as a thinking animal, conscious of his self, began pondering over not only his own development but also the development of the associative ambience he was living in.

While engaged in this process, he eventually realized that for this it was necessary to evolve some means by which the conduct of all the people could be oriented to the goal of a stable, effective and ordered associative living. But how? To find that out, he looked at nature and discovered that the entire natural world goes by an unwritten rule of discipline to which everything of this world is subjected. It was a rule of discipline in the sense that it involved a kind of self-regulation on the part of all. It was corroborated by the evident fact that among all animals, whether carnivorous or herbivorous, and plants as well, a rule prevails that none of a particular species does any harm to others belonging to the same species (although a tiger sometimes kills its cub to satisfy its hunger, but that is an exception and not the general rule); a big tree does not mind the growth of small plants underneath and sometimes gives them necessary support to develop; and so on. From his observation to this effect, man learnt that some unwritten rules, as in the world of nature, might prevail among them too, resting the associative living on cooperation and coexistence. This is how unwritten customs and usages came in vogue in man's associative living. Thus, the rudimentary society of man took a better shape as, with people willing to follow faithfully the unwritten rules or customs, it became more orderly.

At a much later stage, man having had a more developed mind came to the realization that mutual cooperation, assistance and so on, on the basis of which his associative living, subjected to unwritten rules, was running, required him to develop a sense of responsibility and to accept some duties to others. That is, he felt that as he needed help and cooperation from others, the latter also needed the same from him. Man this way became a socially responsible animal,

Notes

conscious of his duties to others. But, as at that stage there was no leader or, for that matter, no one was recognized as superior to others, there was naturally no one to impose these duties on man and to enforce obligation in respect of such duties. Actually, the source of these duties was man's rational consideration or moral conscience, as it came to be known later. From this historical fact, several conclusions may be deduced. First, duty evolved among mankind as innate, not having any external source. This proves that Kant's 'categorical imperative', emphasizing duty as inherent in man's moral self, cannot, after all, be dismissed as pure nonsense. Second, it is seen that the idea of man's duties evolved much earlier than the concept of his rights. Thus, the oft-said statement following from T. H. Green's famous dictum, rights imply duties, is not true, at least chronologically. Third, at that stage of social development, man's duty, with none to enforce, implied a kind of man's moral obligation to others. Thus, man's duty resulted in the germination of morals in man.

With the development of morals, man tended to be more rational, sensible and civilized, although in the earlier phase of associative living he followed no norms in his personal life and also believed in no permanent relation. Accordingly, he indulged in free sex without caring for who his partner was and accepted no responsibility on that score. But now he realized that if he had a moral obligation to others, who together with himself constituted the associative living, he had a moral obligation to himself as well. That is, he felt that personally he had a duty to live and behave in such a way that his way of life could definitively differentiate himself from the rest of the animals. It was out of this moral sense of man that finally originated the institution of family. Once this family had evolved, there came about a lot of changes in the life of man. First, he abjured whatever undisciplined bohemianism he practised earlier. He now had a wife and children whom he regarded as his own to the exclusion of others and had a permanent shelter which he used to call his home. Second, as a family man he accepted certain responsibilities towards his family. He now recognized that it was his duty to protect and care for his family. Third, previously he did not really know what love was. But now, constant companionship of the family members developed in him love, attachment and sympathy. That is, his human and emotional instincts now matured. Last, as soon as man grew a family, he found that he could claim his wife and children exclusively as his own and this is what led to the development of his sense of possession. This sense of possession of man, together with his efforts to collect and store things necessary for maintaining his family, eventually gave birth to the system of property.

EVOLUTION OF SOCIETY

With the development of family and property, society became much different from what it was prior to this development. Since there were now too many families, chances of conflict between them and also within them were very much there. Again, society was now no longer individual-centred, it had to be family-oriented; that is, it was now regarded as constituted by families. As a result, society underwent changes in various ways. First, for the first time, it took a definable and consolidated shape. Second, since property by nature takes various forms, society now became agog with activities, thereby inviting too many complexities, conflicts and troubles.

To cope with this situation, society developed a set of rules, some relating to family, some to property and some others to disputes and conflicts, both within and outside families. These rules were not made by someone; they just grew over the times out of the willingness of people to live along with their families in peace. Yet peace was often elusive and that was entirely due to the system of property. Property is a kind of thing which inevitably leads one in possession of it to have more of it. Thus, everyone at that stage of social development tried to grab as much property as possible, obviously at the cost of others. This naturally intensified disputes and conflicts in society. To combat it, so was felt by all, it was necessary to have a leader of the society, either a single individual or a group of individuals, to regulate all so that the latter would keep their conflicts under restraint. Thus emerged the social leadership and social control. It is not that people living in society by virtue of an agreement among themselves selected an individual or a group of individuals as their leader in consideration of his or their physical prowess (as highlighted by Hobbes, a 17th-century English philosopher). Actually, this leadership spontaneously developed in a person or a group of persons just because they had the qualities and skills to provide leadership. Nobody enthroned them; they enthroned themselves by virtue of their ability.

Marked by social leadership and social control, modern society emerged at last, and once it came into being, it began expanding fast. The expansion, however, was not territorial, but functional. It was functional in the sense that society was now permeated with numerous activities. The continuous expansion of such activities was mainly due to family and property. Family, as noted earlier, generated a sense of possession which ultimately led to the development of property system. Property, by itself, brought in too many activities that entailed too many complications. Hence arose the need of some supreme authority that would force all to obey rules which, again, to facilitate universal and unfailing obedience to them, needed to be codified. It was against the background of such necessity that the State with its codified laws evolved side by side with society.

STATE AND SOCIETY

The modern history of mankind presents this scenario. So, we now have a society with no territory and no government, and a State with a fixed territory and a government and supreme power popularly known as sovereignty. The State has the right to exercise its power belonging overall to society and it can even coerce

Notes

them, if necessary. Thus, the authority of the State has curbed the autonomy of society which the latter had enjoyed for long prior to the emergence of the State. Does it then mean that the State is entitled to control fully every aspect of social life? What exactly should be the relation between the State and the society?

If the issue is viewed through the kaleidoscope of history, it is found that in ancient Greece, the boundaries of the city state prevailing at that time coincided with the boundaries of society. This explains why Plato and Aristotle, the two great masters of Greek political thought, made no differentiation between the State and society. During the Roman rule, however, society was separated from the State. But the Roman rulers were so much preoccupied with the valour of the State that they hardly paid any attention to the proper development of society. So the question of the autonomy of society was just bypassed. In the Mediaeval period, the European society was of course differentiated from the State, but the latter along with the former was completely subjected to overbearing religious authority, that is, the authority of the Church of Rome in such a manner that neither the State nor the society could claim to have any autonomy.

In the light of secularism brought in by the European Renaissance, when Machiavelli and Bodin in the 16th century tried to strengthen the authority of the State, they surely did not deny the separate existence of society. However, there was no attempt on their part to strengthen the base of the society. At last, society vis-à-vis the State was clearly recognized as a separate entity when in the 17th-century England, philosopher John Locke built up the theoretical foundation of liberalism and indirectly mooted the idea that a State is liberal when it leaves the area of society untouched and uninterfered. Following Locke, it may rightly be argued that an essential characteristic of a liberal State is that it will recognize the separate existence of the corresponding society, respect its autonomy and will not interfere with any aspect of society unless it is necessary in the general interest. The liberal State in the advanced Western countries more or less follows this principle. For instance, in the USA or Britain, the State hardly plays any role in the domain of social relations and social activities. This has made the society there extremely powerful in the sense that social groups generally known as interest groups often influence the decision-making process of political authority, though to maintain the purity of their social character, they are least interested to get into the corridors of political power.

Unfortunately, the scenario is altogether different as far as the liberal States of Third World countries are concerned. To illustrate, we may cite the case of India. Viewed from any angle, India undoubtedly is a liberal State. Its authority is based on popular will; it has a democratic political structure; it grants freedom and rights to the people, and honours popular sovereignty. However, the undeniable fact is that the Indian society enjoys very little of autonomy. Here, the controlling arm of political masters, particularly of the ruling party, extends to every corner of the society. This is because of the fact that the only goal of political masters is to win elections, and they seem to be convinced that the shortcut to reach this goal is to establish their dominance through trusted agents in every sphere of the society.

But if in a liberal political system, society is subjected to political control, it in effect harms the State, for the liberal State is then disgraced as it shockingly deviates from the fundamentals of the liberal State. But what is more important is that the society thus unarmed gradually transforms the liberal State into a very weak State, for a liberal society autonomous within its own domain is the source of strength of the liberal State, as it sustains the latter in its functional role, on the basis of its independent judgement, constantly communicates to it the ground realities which help the State decide what to do and what not to do, and, above all, sends signals of warning to the State by means of criticism when the latter falters in its performance or tends to overdo or overstep.

Thus, the copybook comparison between the State and society on the basis of the argument that the State has sovereign power and society does not, and hence the State is more important than the society, makes no sense at all, at least in a liberal system. Indeed, a liberal State is also incomplete and ineffective without a liberal society which cannot flourish unless its autonomy is recognized by the State. Thus, in the context of the liberal system, the society is as much important as the State, and as the State is sovereign, similarly the society is also independent in its own area.

Further, it is agreed by all today that a liberal State must be a pluralist one, and society, undoubtedly, is the breeding ground of this pluralism. Above all, society, no doubt, is the sum total of the individuals living in it. A modern State, particularly whenever it is a liberal State, is committed to securing the freedom of the individual. But denial of the independence of society amounts to denial of the freedom of the individual, which in effect leads to the burial of liberalism. Incidentally, it has long been a practice of the social scientists to demarcate State and society, treating the former as the subject of study of political science and the latter as chiefly the concern of sociology. But in the light of what has been discussed earlier, it may be said that political science should not make any watertight division between State and society, and should treat both as its equal concern.

The history of the evolution of society through ages reveals that until the European Renaissance, human society underwent a process of natural growth; that is, it naturally evolved and was not developed or changed by deliberate efforts. But after the Renaissance had enabled man to discover himself, the

Notes

strength of his arms and the power of his intellect, he took upon himself the task of effecting social change. Thus, society now began changing fast in structure and character by virtue of man's inventive and innovative capacity, thereby establishing that man is the maker of social change. This, of course, does not mean that an individual or a group of individuals one day decides that there should be a change of society and thus the phenomenon of social change takes place. Things are not as easy or as celestial as that.

Actually what happens is that an outstanding thinker or a group of thinkers conceives of an idea, makes some discovery or invents a device which may not attract people of his contemporary society, immediately, in most cases. But gradually, in course of time, people are swayed by the idea and feel inclined to embrace the changes it entails. On the other hand, a device invented or a thing discovered may presuppose spectacular changes in society, but people may initially be incapable of understanding their far-reaching implications. But when the device or discovery, through scientific activities, unfurls its potentialities of social change, people obviously find themselves in the midst of the sea of social changes. To illustrate, when Dalhousie introduced railways in British India, Karl Marx, living far away from this country, predicted spectacular social change in the then India. Eventually, in course of time, this prediction came true. Again, when in the West steam power and atom were discovered, people could not immediately foresee the changes in society these would bring about. But today, everybody can see how much of social change is due to that discovery.

A modern State, it is found, is often keen on bringing about social change, and it cannot be denied that it becomes successful too. In fact, one of the main objectives of a modern liberal democratic State is to take up various egalitarian measures to ameliorate the living conditions of the downtrodden. If these measures succeed, then certainly the society changes structurally. But the State can hardly change the social milieu which can only be changed by society itself, that is, when the people constituting society voluntarily accept a behavioural, attitudinal and cultural change. So, in the ultimate analysis, it is not the State but the society which is the main actor in social change.

3 CHAPTER

The State

Notes

INTRODUCTION

In the second half of the 20th century, the exponents of the empirical approach to politics decided to do away with the concept of the State. Pre-eminent among them was David Easton, the apostle of systems analysis, who mooted that there had been available until his time 135 'definitions' of the State, resulting in the impossibility of producing a general theory of politics. Accordingly, he felt that time had come to abjure the idea of the State and replace it by a new concept. The immediate reaction was much favourable. Many of the political scientists, including those of the Third World such as India, felt elated at this development and were convinced that a new era had dawned in the world of political science. Following suit, it may be noted that quite a few political scientists in the closing years of the last century developed theories on what they called the 'roll back' of the State. Yet the common political parlance has not yet been able to get rid of the term 'State' and this is what justifies the title of this piece. The use of the term 'State' may thus be acceptable, but what can hardly be accepted is the attempt on the part of many, particularly the textbook writers of India, to spend quite a lot of space in discussing elaborately what they define as theories regarding the origin of the State, for none of these theories was ever intended, in fact, to go into the origin of the State. Their purpose was only to enquire into the basis of the authority of the State, to explain why on earth people living in a State voluntarily render their obedience to the State.

Notes

Indeed it is pointless to develop any theory of the origin of the State, for the State in any case did not originate at a particular point of time. Like society, it gradually evolved over the times. Of course it was born out of society. As we have seen earlier, society, at a certain stage of its development, developed certain unwritten rules to be followed by everyone for the sake of sustenance of social life. Initially, everything went on well with these rules. But as time went by, it was found that more and more a tendency was growing among the people to violate these rules, resulting in chaos and disorder in social life. In the face of this situation, people realized that this violation was due to the fact that there was none to give any punishment for such violation. Thus was felt the necessity for having someone as their leader, who could regulate their personal and social behaviour, force them to follow the rules and punish them for breach of these rules. The moment this leader emerged with his coercive powers, the State in a rudimentary form came into being.

However, the leader whose emergence indicated the insemination of the State was not made, but born. That is, he was not selected by the people around by means of their free and deliberate choice. He made himself a leader by virtue of some of his qualities which, without doubt, established his superiority over others. The qualities, of course, were of varying kinds. Sometimes, it was his masterly skill in collecting the means of livelihood for others or his greater command over the possession of property or just his magical power to mesmerize others and so on. In any case, it was his extraordinary personal qualities that made him a leader with unquestioning authority over others. All this did not happen in a single day. It took ages for the leader to establish his lordship over others. However, once this authority was consolidated, it did not take too long for it to assume an institutional form and that form was monarchy armed with personal supremacy which much later theoretically came to be known as sovereignty.

Thus, after the ancient Greek period in European history, the State took a definitive shape with a monarchical government at the top of its realm. Since from the very beginning it carried along with it the attribute of indomitable authority over others, it came to be regarded as a kind of entity with none to control it from above; that is, as propounded for the first time by Bodin, a 16th-century French philosopher, it came to be characterized by sovereignty. The sovereignty of the State which thus initially remained personal, through ages of struggle and movement, particularly the 17th-century Puritan Revolution and Glorious Revolution taking place in England, finally reached out to the people and took the form of popular sovereignty, theoretically conceptualized by the 18th-century philosopher Rousseau.

This change in the wielder of supreme power inevitably led to the change of government. Monarchy was now replaced by democracy, a form of government

Notes

where people are supposed to be the source of sovereign power, and, needless to add, it is this democracy that happens to be the order of the day in modern times. Naturally, modern political scientists are found to view the democratic State from various angles, to talk about uses and misuses of democracy, and to produce very many theories of democracy. Above all, there are few countries in the modern world where people in general as well as political scientists and political observers do not give three cheers for democracy as the best form of government—so far, so good. However, we cannot possibly avoid two very pertinent questions: (a) Is the State a concrete reality? (b) Is democracy possible?

The State, in fact, is an intangible entity which can only be felt but hardly empirically tested. To put it differently, it is a generic term symbolizing the totality of political functions at various levels used for the sake of theoretical convenience, but not a concrete reality, or, at best, is a Platonic reality beyond the world of senses. Its people can be seen, its territory may be measured and its government is very much found to be at work. But its sovereignty which happens to be its chief characteristic, like it, cannot be seen. Further, whenever sovereignty is personal as in a monarchical system, it can be easily located. In fact, in a system of singular rule such as monarchy or dictatorship, one person holds the reins and everything runs at his behest. His words are law and so indisputably he is the sovereign. But in a democracy, it is rather difficult to locate sovereignty, for people who are claimed to be sovereign in a democracy are, in actual practice, far from so. Again, if it is argued that in a democracy the State represents the people and hence the State holds sovereignty on behalf of the people, then the questions that invariably arise are as follows: (a) Where is the State? (b) How to locate it objectively?

One may try to resolve this quandary by arguing that at least in a parliamentary form of democracy there is a clear answer to this question, as in a parliamentary democracy, parliament decidedly is sovereign. But still the question remains, for, as everybody knows, in a parliamentary democracy the system of majority rule largely curbs the supreme power of parliament as the executive there, backed up by majority party in parliament, usurps virtually the whole of parliament's constituent and legislative power. Thus, in actual practice, parliament there is hardly sovereign. There may be a counterargument that if in a parliamentary system sovereignty does not reside where it is theoretically supposed to be, at least in a presidential democracy like the USA, sovereignty can very definitely be located, for in the USA, federal supreme court with no one above to control it, and independent of the legislature and the executive, can freely work and nullify any law made by the US Congress just on the grounds, that it is unfair and unreasonable and does not have to care for the colossal authority of the US president. Yet it is not really sovereign, for it is the president who appoints the judges of the Supreme Court, subject to approval by the

Notes

Senate, the upper house of the US Congress. Thus, the US federal Supreme Court can, by no means, be regarded as a sovereign body. In other words, the location of sovereignty also poses a problem in a presidential democracy like that of the USA. Hence, to the first question, the answer must be that far from being a concrete reality, the State is a theoretical construct necessary, of course, for any discussion on politics. Similarly, sovereignty being an essential characteristic of the State cannot really be located among the people within the democratic framework, thereby implying perhaps that in the democratic world of concrete reality, the State indeed is non-existent.

Now to the second question, that is, the question about the possibility of democracy. Born in the 17th-century England, democracy has gone through many trials and errors, and despite many challenges, both theoretical and ideological, it has well survived till now. Not only that, those who favour it claim that it represents historic triumph of the people as in this form of government, people, in the ultimate analysis, are the final arbiter with the sovereignty of the State vested in them. True, in a democratic system, people by means of periodic elections take a leading role in the formation of government. To that extent they are, of course, sovereign. But once the government is constituted, it disavows any accountability to the people and takes decisions on its own. Rousseau indeed was right when he remarked that in a democracy like England, people are sovereign only for one day, that is, on the day of election. It may be argued, however, that at least in a parliamentary democracy, the legislature is constituted by the representatives of the people and it is to this body that the Council of Ministers including the prime minister remains accountable, thereby implying that this accountability, in the ultimate analysis, is to the people. But unfortunately, development of a highly organized party system has mostly messed up this accountability or, for that matter, sovereignty of the people because an executive having absolute majority in the legislature completely dominates the latter and virtually moves it in the way it wishes. But how to identify the State? Where is it to be found? Again, if in reality the State cannot be traced out, then who is sovereign? Where is it to be located? As shown above, these are the awesome riddles of political science.

THE IDEA OF STATE AND RELATED RIDDLES

Unfortunately, none of the modern political scientists has ever tried to solve these riddles. On the contrary, by means of their theoretical sophistication, some of them have brought in newer complications. To illustrate, we may refer to David Easton's systems model. Disgusted with the term 'State' and keen on producing a general theory of politics applicable to all countries, irrespective of

Notes

whatever form of government they have, Easton brings to the focus political system as the principal subject of enquiry and analysis in political science. His model of political system is based on input–output analysis, which in simple words means that demands from the clientele (which means actually the people living under a political system), after proper articulation, reach the decision-makers in the form of input which then at that level undergoes conversion process and reaches the clientele in the form of output, that is, decision. The clientele may adversely react to some of these decisions which again, through a process of feedback, reach the decision-makers who accordingly change their earlier decisions. In this way, Easton shows that the process continuously goes on cyclically.

Unfortunately, Easton's model is just idealistic and simplistic as well, for in a democratic system, particularly a democratic system of most of the Third World countries, it is a commonplace that power often does not care for popular will and desire while taking decisions. Further, when a decision is disliked by the people, it rarely happens that the political decision-maker changes its decision as per the demand of the people. Thus, Easton's input–output model as well as those emulating it are all abstracted from reality. This perhaps explains why in our time the common folk often complain that there is always a huge gap between the theory and practice of politics.

Again, according to Easton, the major function of the political system is to make 'authoritative allocation of values in a society'. That is, whatever allocation of values is made is mandatory for all; no one has the right to go against it. But the questions that immediately come up are as follows: Why on earth the clientele will take it as authoritative? How can he who makes this allocation claim it to be authoritative? On what grounds? Easton has no answer to these questions. It may be surmised with reason that although Easton rejects the State, he has very much in mind the sovereignty of the State while he uses the term 'authoritative'. However, he does not admit that perhaps because of his apprehension that acknowledgement of sovereignty in his theory will amount to inviting the State through the backdoor, and will, in effect, affect the novelty and modernity of his theory.

This really is the problem with the post-war modern political scientists. They produce theories which, no doubt, are qualitatively and methodically distinctive. But they hardly bother what may be the possible implications of such theories. Moreover, in their craze to produce something novel, they seem to be least concerned that the theories they construct are fully related to the realities of life. This is probably because of their conviction that theory is for theory's sake and that a theoretician is not obliged at all to give due attention to the niceties of real life.

Notes

STATE, SOVEREIGNTY AND GOVERNMENT

If, however, the theory of politics is to be taken out of the shell of so-called modern theoretical acrobatics and linked to realities of life, then political science, as is in vogue, will need a drastic surgery. This will mean a little change in attitude, envisaging dropping of a few terms, reconstruction of some concepts and bringing in new meaning to some others. In the context of this changed attitude, the first casualty will, of course, be the State. The term 'State', first coined in the early 16th century by Machiavelli, has been in use for hundreds of years. But, as noted earlier, it is essentially a theoretical construct surely helpful for theoretical discussions, but not felt or visible in real life. What can be seen in real life is that in a country, there are people living in a territory with fixed and identifiable boundaries, and a government at work, whatever its form. It is also seen that such people have a conscious and an intense sense of belonging to their country, which is signified by the territory they live in, together with its history, ethos and culture. This sense of belonging, after it takes a concentrated form, assumes the name of nationalism, and once this nationalism is developed, the country concerned together with its people goes by the name of the nation. Thus, in reality, what we find in a country is that there is a nation, a government and, of course, sovereignty, as without it a nation cannot claim to be independent. So it seems that in real life, we can very well go without the State, the pet term of a good many political theorists for ages. However, it may be asked: If the State is abdicated in political discourse then sovereignty being traditionally regarded as the most important characteristic of the State, whereon will it repose and what will be its destination? The answer to this question may be like this: Notwithstanding the traditional exponents of sovereignty who view it as indivisible, in reality sovereignty is divisible. Sovereignty is both internal and external. The internal sovereignty is of course indivisible and, in actual practice, government alone is sovereign since it can make and unmake many things, disregarding the legislature in both parliamentary and presidential forms of democracy, and even when judiciary is powerful enough to stall some of its moves by its judgement, it can overcome this judgement by means of constitutional amendment or fresh legislation. There are plenty of such instances in the political history of the Indian Republic. Further, the government holds the highest coercive power and is entitled to exercise it not only against aggression or invasion but also internally over the citizens and aliens. Thus, it becomes clear that what Bodin called 'absolute power' lies not with the illusive State but with the government which is tangible and visible in all its actions.

The government is internally sovereign, no doubt. But it cannot claim external sovereignty, as it will be too much for it to assert its sovereignty over governments of other countries. Viewed from this angle, the government's sovereignty is not total and indivisible. Who then enjoys external sovereignty? It may be said

Notes

that actually it is the nation which is externally sovereign. Because the nation alone may assert its autonomy and independence against other nations. This is why the world body which is at work for more than six decades is called the United Nations (UN). The duty of the government in respect to the nation is to protect its sovereignty. Thus, the government does not enjoy external sovereignty. It serves as the sentinel of external sovereignty of the nation.

To the traditionalists, the idea that the government and not the State is sovereign may sound preposterous. But interestingly, a corroboration to that effect may be found in the theory of Austin who is traditionally accepted as a pioneer in defining sovereignty. While defining sovereignty, Austin lays emphasis on a determinate human superior. To quote him, 'If a determinate human superior, not in the habit of obedience to a like superior, receives habitual obedience from the bulk of a given society, that determinate superior is sovereign' (*Lectures on Jurisprudence*, 1873). The State surely fails this criterion as it cannot be equated to a determinate human superior. On the other hand, government, which is a body of human superiors, surely meets this requirement. Further, the enormity of power of the government is clearly visible. True, in a democratic system, government is subject to the ordinary and fundamental laws of the land, that is, the constitution. But it implies only its obligation to follow the rule of law which characterizes a democracy, particularly the parliamentary democracy. It is in no way a hindrance against the exercise of its supreme power.

If this sovereign government in action is empirically observed, it will be seen that it is viewed diversely by people, that is, it appears with different images to different kinds of people. This is especially so in a country like India where there is a huge number of illiterate or semi-literate people or rural population living far away from the seat of governmental power. Their perception of government is much different from that of those who are educated, well informed and urbanized. Thus, to an ignorant villager, a government tax collector or a petty government official serving the rural area is government, as his knowledge and communication are limited only to that. Similarly, in an urban area, to a rickshaw puller, a traffic guard or police constable represents the sovereign government, as his interaction does not go beyond that. Even in an advanced country like Britain, to a little educated old lady, the queen is the government, since all her life she has been engrossed in her love and reverence for the queen, taking the latter as the symbol of sovereign ruler. This is how people representing different walks of life perceive government differently. However, they all agree in their belief that government is the most powerful agency in the country with none above to control it. Hence, it may be said that people, a delimited territory, a sovereign government and a nation are the four elements of a country.

If the government is taken to be sovereign, one may ask, will it not indulge in political absolutism? The apprehension however is baseless, for sovereignty

Notes

does not presuppose arbitrariness, at least in a democratic system. As noted above, the sovereign government has to work always subject to the constitution and law, and hence there is little chance of its being wayward. There may be a further question as well. What is the position of the individual vis-à-vis the sovereign government. The answer is not difficult to find out. The relation between the two is that of mutual services. The individual is obliged to serve the government in the form of obeying its laws and orders, and of acting and behaving in such a way that the sovereignty of the government is by no means affected and the order in society established by the government is not disrupted in any way. On the other hand, it is the duty of the government as the supreme public body to serve the individual by way of ensuring his welfare, looking after his interest and facilitating his wholesome development. These are the tasks which presuppose the functions of government as a governing agency. The government, therefore, is duty-bound to render these services to the individual. But why is the individual obliged to obey the government? That is, what are the grounds of political obligation? This indeed is one of the perennial questions of political science.

OBEDIENCE TO STATE

Why does the individual citizen consider it his duty to obey the State? It is around this question that the theory of political obligation has developed. Political obligation, it may be mentioned, is different from political obedience. When people obey the State, it is political obedience. When they feel obliged to obey the State (government in our parlance presented above), it is political obligation. Thus, political obedience is a sheer fact independent of any normative connotation, while political obligation involves a sense of duty, a normative function.

Philosophers of the world have pondered over this question for ages. Aristotle, one of the two great masters of ancient Greek political thought, first tried to give an answer to the question. True, he did not directly deal with the question. However, implicit in his theory is the proposition that as man is by nature a political animal, he has no other choice than to submit to the authority of the State. The proposition is actually a statement of fact, but hardly an explanation. That is, Aristotle gives a very simple answer, but he fails to provide any rationale for political obedience. In other words, he enquires into political obedience but not political obligation.

If Aristotle's answer was simple, much simpler was the answer of most of the mediaeval writers of Europe. According to them, as political authority represents the authority of God on earth, obeying the State is nothing but obeying God. This is a kind of explanation that takes it for granted that obeying God is imperative and hence obeying the State is imperative as well. This is virtually a restatement of Aristotle's argument that man is under compulsion to obey the State. Yet it should be mentioned that there is a normative element involved in it, for, saturated in religion, these mediaeval thinkers were led by the belief that everyone has a fundamental duty to obey God and his agents. Thus, indirectly they touched upon political obligation.

In the post-Renaissance Europe, the 17th-century English philosopher Hobbes was the first thinker to deal with the grounds of political obedience. One of the conclusions of his social contract theory is that man obeys the State because the latter gives him security of his life and property. This implies that man is afraid of a situation where he will feel insecure and unsafe. Further, Hobbes argues that the State is a 'Leviathan' armed with massive power. Obviously, he means to say that the individual, afraid of the power of the State, surrenders to this 'Leviathan'. If fear is, thus, the basis of political obedience, then it may be said that although not directly like Aristotle, but at least indirectly, Hobbes too postulates that there is no other choice for the individual than to obey the State.

Locke, another social contract theorist and 17th-century English philosopher like Hobbes, provides a different argument. According to him, man as human being inheres some rights such as the rights to life, liberty and property, and he obeys the State as it protects these rights. These actually are basic human rights without which an individual cannot live as a true human being and, needless to say, everyone would like to be a human being and not a beast. Hence, for protection of his human rights he must turn to the State, having no other choice, and as the State alone can protect these rights he has no other choice than to obey the State. Thus, apparently, both Hobbes and Locke are advocates of non-optional political obedience. However, on two counts Locke's theory has merits not shared by that of Hobbes. First, according to him, the three basic rights of the individual are absolutely his own and not the creation of the State. He also stresses that the State, notwithstanding having more power than the individual, cannot at all invade or interfere with these rights. Thus, he earmarks a sphere for the individual where the latter enjoys absolute autonomy against the State. Second, he argues that if the State fails in its duty to protect the basic rights of the individual, the latter has every right to resist the State and replace those who run the State. Hence, it may rightly be concluded that Locke's State is not as absolute as the Hobbesian 'Leviathan'. Further, according to him, the individual's duty to obey the State is coupled with the latter's duty to protect the rights of the former. This clearly amounts to saying that obedience rendered by the individual to the State is not absolute but conditional.

To the question why the individual obeys the State, the answer of Rousseau, an 18th-century social contract theorist, is however somewhat different. By posing the State as the embodiment of general will, he argues that while obeying

Notes

the State, the individual actually obeys the general will and because the general will includes the will of the individual, in obeying the State the individual virtually obeys himself. The explanation, no doubt, is a novel one. But, unfortunately, the concept of general will is nebulous. Indeed, Rousseau fails to provide any plausible criterion for determining the general will. Naturally, his attempt to account for political obedience falls through. However, Rousseau's general will is generally acclaimed as the root of the idea of popular sovereignty which serves as the basis of democracy.

Hegel, the great German philosopher, presents a peculiar argument on the issue. According to him, the State is the embodiment and actualization of freedom. Therefore, if the individual is willing to enjoy freedom, he has to obey the State. Since every individual likes to live as a free animal, freedom is one of his prime necessities. But, as Hegel is convinced, for meeting this necessity, it is compulsive for the individual to obey the State. In the ultimate analysis, it means that, according to Hegel, obedience is virtually mandatory for the individual. This obviously provides no answer to the question why the individual chooses to obey the State.

To the early empiricists such as David Hume and Jeremy Bentham, on the other hand, obedience is clearly prudential. That is, the individual obeys the State just because it is advantageous for him to do so. This, no doubt, is an honest attempt to account for political obedience. But its main defect is that it cannot be universally applied, for there may be some who may argue that they do not find any advantage in obeying the authority of the State and hence they may refuse to obey. But political obedience is a universal fact; that is, whether one may like it or not, political obedience, like many other things, is part of one's life. From this standpoint, prudential explanation of political obedience is incomplete and inadequate. Besides, prudential obligation is no obligation at all, for to do what is to one's advantage does not involve any sense of duty and hence it cannot be called obligation. So prudential obligation is also defective.

T. H. Green, a 19th-century English political philosopher, provides a moral explanation of the grounds of political obligation. According to him, the State is contributory to the moral development of the individual and, in view of this, for the sake of his moral development, the individual obeys the State. Apparently, this is quite a plausible explanation as Green adduces a definitive reason behind political obedience. Besides, Green unlike his predecessors clearly focuses on political obligation, for his theory envisages a duty of the individual to obey the State. Because it may be said, the individual has a duty to ensure his moral development and as the State is instrumental to his moral development, he feels it his duty to obey the State. This is why Green's theory was accepted for long as a valid theory of political obligation. But it may be added that Green's explanation takes it for granted that every individual is keen on having his moral development, an assumption which does not agree with the concrete facts of life. In real life, it is rarely found that an ordinary mortal, unless of course he is a godly one, actually looks for his moral development. Thus, Green's analysis does not apply generally but only in exceptional cases.

Notes

CONCLUDING OBSERVATIONS

As noted earlier, the State is just a theoretical construct. In actual practice, the State is nothing but the government. Therefore, in reality the individual obeys not the State but the government. The government functions mainly through laws and orders. Hence, political obedience actually amounts to obeying the laws and orders of the government. The question that is of relevance then is: Why does an individual obey government's laws and orders? The government is an organization different from others in that it alone possesses coercive power, which it applies through its various agencies. Thus, it can give punishment if someone refuses to obey its laws and orders or openly violates any of them. Does it mean then that the individual obeys the diktat of the government just because he is afraid of its coercive power? This may be true in case of an autocratic government which overtly rules by force, that is, where people are forced to obey the government. But this does not hold well in the case of a modern democratic government which, although armed with force, rarely uses it. What is usually found in a modern democracy is that barring a few miscreants who deliberately violate laws and are punished for their offence, people generally obey laws without being asked by the government or by anyone else to do so. In other words, their obedience is voluntary and spontaneous. This is due to their realization that abiding by laws in vogue is part of their civilized living based on peace and order to maintain which is one of the principal tasks of the laws of government. Thus, one of the possible reasons behind political obedience may be the fact that people are deeply fond of having a civilized life. But this is not the only reason behind the grounds of political obedience. There are other reasons as well.

The individual as a human being, it may be noted, obeys many other things besides the laws of government. Thus, he obeys the laws of nature as he knows that he cannot change these laws and accordingly he prefers to remain loyal to such laws. Again, as a social animal he follows the customs and usages prevailing in society. Naturally, he follows the uncoded norms regulating social relations. Similarly, within the family, he obeys his superiors and does not go against the family rules and norms. Thus, it may be said that obedience lies in the very nature of man. However, this does not really explain political obedience, for in

Notes

other cases noted above the individual has a direct involvement in what he obeys. But as far as government is concerned, he has little involvement, except in case of his casting votes in periodic elections in a democratic system. Further, in relation to government, the individual is not just a human being but more a political animal. So what he does as a human being does not necessarily apply to him when he is in the role of a political animal. Hence, the explanation that the very nature of man is to obey is not enough to account for political obedience.

It may be said that obedience is actually a product of man's socialization. When a child begins growing up, he starts learning many things within the family. He develops the habit of obeying the rules of the family. Nobody tells him to do so. He develops these habits on his own. Later, as a member of peer groups, he develops more of this habit. In schools and colleges also, he learns to obey many things. Further, as a member of society, he develops civic habits that help him obey the social norms and rules. Finally, as a political animal, that is, as a citizen, following others, he develops the habit of obeying the laws of government. The government on its part does neither force him nor ask him to obey its orders and laws. The individual submits to them as a matter of habit. But if it is taken that man as a political animal or, for that matter, as a citizen obeys the government as a matter of habit, then the question that is unavoidable is: How others from whom a particular individual has learnt the habit of political obedience have developed this habit? In other words, there is no clear answer to the question, what is the root of this habit of regarding it as a duty to obey the government. Indeed, to say that the individual is habitually obedient to government involves the fallacy of begging question.

In real life, whatever appears to be the shortcoming of a democratic political system, it cannot after all be denied that unlike an autocratic government, it is not power-oriented, but service-oriented. Indeed, the main objective of a democratic government is to render services to the people. Hence, most of the laws of government in a democracy are meant to serve the people. However, the government while giving these services expects that people will bear a cost for them, and that cost is obedience. People on their part willingly take it as their duty to obey the government along with its laws and orders as they realize that it is their obedience that makes the laws viable and if the laws fail to operate in the absence of obedience, then they will be the ultimate losers as they will be denied the services by the laws.

Thus, political obligation in the final analysis is a matter of mutual benefit. Without it the laws of government make no sense. Similarly, without it there is hardly any benefit in the life of the individual. However, to realize that laws are meant to do good to the individuals, what is needed is appropriate civic and political consciousness. The ignorant and the illiterate cannot be expected to obey consciously. They obey the laws because they just learn it from others' examples. As far as they are concerned, political obligation is a result of socialization. In other cases, political obligation is based on political consciousness. Only conscious political animals are aware of the values of the laws of government, and hence they spontaneously regard it as their duty to obey these laws. For the rest, it is a matter of learnt practice.

4

CHAPTER

The Civil Society

Notes

INTRODUCTION

As shown earlier, society is no less important than the State. The society evolved much earlier than the State, and the latter was born out of the former. Further, society sustains the State in that it adds strength to the State. In fact, how the State will work depends much on the type of society it is based on. Thus, the character of a democratic State is determined largely by the nature of a democratic society. However, with the emergence of sociology as a separate discipline dealing exclusively with society, the latter was taken out of the province of political science. From then onwards, political science began evolving the concept of civil society and theorizing on it, although the idea of civil society was incidentally touched on much earlier than the birth of sociology.

As regards civil society, the primary question is: Is civil society a part of the State or is independent of the State? On this question, there are varying opinions, particularly among the three leading groups of theoreticians. For instance, Hegel who for the first time brought the idea of civil society to the focus and developed a theory on it, regarded civil society as very much different from the State. According to him, civil society represents an intermediate phase in the evolution of the State. To him, structurally and qualitatively civil society is much higher than the family, an institution growing in the initial stage of the historical process of development of the State, marked by perfect unity. It is also higher than the family, in the sense that it is permeated by diverse economic activities. Yet it is a social form much inferior to the State. However, conflict of economic activities impedes unity in the civil society, which according to Hegel makes it far short of an institution having complete fulfilment. The State, on the contrary, represents a synthesis of the attributes of family and civil society. That is, it combines both unity and diversity, and hence is a complete organization superior to civil society.

The Marxists however view civil society in a completely different way. They all agree that civil society and the State are so integrally related to each other that one cannot be judged independently of the other. Yet they have developed this viewpoint differently. For instance, Karl Marx himself holds the thesis that in a capitalist system, civil society is nothing other than the bourgeois society. He further argues that it is this civil society characterized by its property relations that acts as the base of the corresponding superstructure, that is, the State. Thus, according to Marx it is the base, that is, the civil society, that conditions the character of the State, which on its part applies all its coercive instruments to keep the civil society intact. It appears then that according to Marx the primary task of the State is to be always in the service of the civil society.

Gramsci, another celebrated Marxist, holds almost a contrary opinion. According to him, the State is not in the service of the civil society; rather, the civil society is in the service of the State. The task of the civil society is to guard the State against all attack and help it perpetuate its rule. Thus, Gramsci describes the civil society as a protective ditch around the fortress of the State. No wonder Gramsci suggests that the capture of State power in a capitalist system by way of revolution is not enough to bring in a radical social change. What is required is the complete destruction of the ideational, intellectual and cultural apparatus operative in a civil society that supports and protects the State.

The liberal view of the civil society is, however, altogether different. In fact, the liberals claim that the idea of civil society is a product of liberalism and to trace its roots, one has to go back to the theory of Locke. Locke, of course, did not develop a full-fledged theory of civil society. However, he provided enough materials to construct it. For instance, he made a clear distinction between political society, that is, the State and society as such, which as opposed to political society might be named the civil society, though Locke himself never uses this name. In any case, Locke throughout his theory maintains a clear distinction between the State and society. He shows that society is born out of a freely made contract among people. But by this, only the society came into being and not the State which denotes a much later development. According to Locke, the State is not the result of a voluntary agreement among the people. It is actually the result of a fiduciary trust by means of which people, already having constituted an autonomous society, vest on the State the power to rule. Thus, not the State but the people constituting the society are the final arbiter. That Locke is very serious about maintaining a clear distinction between State and society is further proved by the fact that according to him, whenever the ruler

Notes

representing the State fails in its obligation to fulfil the conditions of the trust by which it has been created, people are entitled to dislodge it and replace it by a new one. However, this political change, Locke makes it clear, does not mean any change in the social framework which remains unchangeable, no matter whatever changes the State undergoes. Locke consistently maintains that there is a clear line of difference between the State and society. This indeed is the starting point of the liberal theory of civil society. However, before we go more into it, it will be better to have a closer look at the theories of civil society as propounded by Marx and Gramsci.

To Marx, civil society is of course independent of the State. However, it has no active role with regard to the State. The task of the State according to Marx is to meet the needs and requirements of the civil society so that the latter is sustained perpetually. This virtually amounts to saying that the State is just a stooge of the civil society. But if it is so, then there is hardly any point in regarding the civil society as independent, for if the civil society is the supreme arbiter of the State then it is just begging the question to say that the civil society is independent of the State. Further, it may be said that Marx's civil society is rather passive in relation to the State, for all its functions are directed to the goal of augmentation of its power and it does not at all struggle for its survival. Whatever struggle is needed in this regard is done on its behalf by the State, which happens to be its handmaid. Above all, in Marx's theory civil society seems to be rather mixed up with the State. Since the former represents the base and the latter the superstructure, they together appear to constitute an integrated whole, creating rather the impression that the State is the civil society and the civil society is the State.

Gramsci's theory of civil society, however, is free from the so-called mix-up of the State and civil society. To him, the State and civil society are distinct from each other and independent of each other. Further, unlike Marx, he argues that civil society tries to protect the State with all its might against all possible onslaught. To this extent, Gramsci's theory is undoubtedly better than that of Marx. However, it may be noted, according to Marx the State may exercise its power including coercive power to any extent to keep the civil society intact. On the other hand, Gramsci's civil society goes to any extent to keep the State extremely powerful. Thus, both the theories smack of a kind of totalitarianism. This is what the liberal theorists, for obvious reasons, cannot put up with and hence their alternative model of civil society.

NATURE OF CIVIL SOCIETY

According to the liberals, society is much wider in area than the State and many of its orbits including social relations; social, cultural and religious activities; and

Notes

customs and traditions are beyond the purview of the State. Thus, society enjoys extensive autonomy and the State a limited authority. It is against this backdrop that the liberals present their theory of civil society. According to the liberals, civil society must not be confused with the whole of society. It is just a part of the society comprising mainly the educated middle class and the social elite. However, it does not automatically by itself become a civil society. To be a civil society, it must be conscious of its own position in society, of its rights, freedom and dignity and must also know what its functions are.

The civil society within the liberal framework is a social organization running parallel to the State and, although having no coercive power like the State, supported by public opinion it can well vie with the political decision-makers whom it can restrain and regulate with its social power, keeping always in view the public interest. In actual practice, it plays the role of an alert sentinel keeping vigil over the performance of the State, cautions the latter in case of its failure or lapses and peacefully agitates whenever the government refuses to rectify itself or goes against the will of the people. However, if this agitation assumes the form of violence or anomie, or if the civil society is interested in entering the corridors of power, it ceases to be a civil society. It then turns into a political party or a frontal organization of a political party.

Actually, the liberal ideal about the power and autonomy of society is well reflected in the civil society. This is why civil society best agrees with the liberal framework. Civil society, it may further be said, is an action group, the functions of which are targeted not only at the State but also the society. That is, civil society is not only active in eradicating the political wrongs but also any social vice. Thus, in the liberal view, civil society is truly independent. It is independent of not only the State but also the society that parents it.

But viability and success of civil society very much depend on the development of a congenial environment. Responsibility on that score lies not only with the State but also with the society and even with the civil society itself. The State has a primary responsibility in this regard. If it chooses to make itself omnipotent, all-pervasive and absolutely interfering leaving little opportunity to the society to enjoy autonomy then the society, highly politicized in effect, fails to create the milieu for the healthy growth of a civil society. As indicated earlier, educated middle class and social elite represent the backbone of a civil society. Hence, in this matter the State has a major responsibility. It should give best efforts towards the spread of education, step up the speed of economic development, generate employment and patronize middle-class culture.

Society, on the other hand, must guard its autonomy at any cost. It should not allow any political interference in the social activities, and for this, it needs to develop public opinion so strong that politics does not dare ignoring and undermining it. Above all, it should create conditions favourable for the

Notes

development of social leadership. True, social leadership like any other leadership is not made but grows spontaneously. However, the strength of this leadership is tested through one's worth and achievement in the area of social activities. Therefore, the larger is the range of such social activities, the greater is the scope of the emergence of social leadership which obviously is at the helm of the civil society.

The civil society itself has no responsibility in this respect. It ought to be cautious in maintaining infrangible cohesion within itself and see to it that there is no internal dissension ruining its strength. This dissension usually takes place when personal ambition, particularly political ambition, of the prominent members of the civil society overtakes their loyalty to the ideal of the civil society. In a developed society where the State is content with its delimited jurisdiction, accepting a clear demarcation between itself and society and never extending its control to the society, and where political power is hardly its overriding object among many other things to aspire after, civil society normally does not have internal dissension nor does it often break down. There civil society naturally is very powerful and the State accords it due recognition. But in underdeveloped societies like India the scenario is altogether different. Here the problem is of various kinds. First, society is not sufficiently developed and modernized to view the State at par with itself. Second, as the State is armed with immense coercive power, society in the face of it takes itself not in any way comparable to the State. Third, as the State holds and wields colossal power, it considers itself an overlord over everything that includes society as well.

CIVIL SOCIETY AND INDIA

A truly liberal State surely does not share this point of view. But in India, for instance, it is otherwise just because of the continued persistence of the colonial heritage. In colonial days, the foreign rulers of India not only held huge power but also looked having almost a royal splendour. Viewing this, people at the receiving end used to regard political power as the most awesome and prized possession in human life. Naturally, after the arrival of independence in India, power hunger among the people rose and the elite of the society became more interested in the State than the society, as power together with its glamour was available only in the domain of the State and not in that of society. Second, this megalomania has led the political parties to act and behave in a manner completely inimical to the liberal principles. Without honouring the autonomy of the society, which they are supposed to do in a liberal system, that is, without caring to foster liberal society, they seek to politicize society as far as possible and whenever any of these parties is able to capture political power, that is, whenever it assumes the role of the ruling party, it aggressively advances to every epicentre of social life and establishes thereon its total control.

Notes

Thus, although a perfectly liberal political system has been at work in India for nearly 70 years, a liberal society with autonomy as its pre-eminent characteristic is yet to evolve. Accordingly, in the absence of favourable conditions for its growth a civil society has not properly developed in India. True, on occasions in the wake of an issue affecting the interests of the people, a civil society suddenly develops, and initially it appears to be quite active and powerful. But gradually it starts losing its strength and finally becomes imbecile. This frequently happens in one or other of the civil societies of India. Further, in the context of a general tendency of the Indian elite to stay close to the corridors of power, it may so happen that the members of civil society eventually turn into a loyal lackey of government, playing the latter's tune. Or maybe members of civil society after enthusiastically carrying on their activities for some time finally fail to overcome the temptation of political power and accordingly get transformed voluntarily into a political party, fighting elections in course of time.

This has often happened in India in the past and is still happening. However, some exceptions to this general trend are also found. Actually, whenever social leadership leading a civil society is extremely strong, dauntless and completely free from political ambition, the civil society led by it moves on the right track and serves well the cause it is committed to. Unfortunately, such instances are few and far between. Usually what happens in India is that social leadership fails to retain its social character for long, eventually yielding to its political aspiration or failing to resist pressure from political parties. As a result, in India civil society is found to exist in a form, but with its spirit very much lost. This emaciated civil society has indeed been affecting the strength of Indian democracy.

CIVIL SOCIETY AND DEMOCRACY

This brings one to the question about the relevance and importance of civil society in a democracy. As seen earlier, although government in a parliamentary democratic system, as in India, is formed by means of popular elections and it accepts its accountability to people's representatives constituting the legislature, in the ultimate analysis it is nothing but an elite government. In the presidential democratic system too, though the chief executive is directly or indirectly elected by people, he and his government comprising his hand-picked individuals as ministers virtually has no accountability to the people. Thus, every form of democratic government represents not popular rule but elite rule. However, this elite government to remain true to the ideal of democracy should be responsive to people and the society they represent. If it is so, then there must be some mechanism through which the responsiveness of the democratic (but elite) government may be meaningfully operative. It is civil society that serves as this mechanism. Indeed democracy and civil society are so integrally related to each other that it is impossible to think of one without the other.

Notes

Democracy, admittedly, is not just a form of government but it also presupposes a way of life. It is not the task of a democratic government to create this way of life. It can at best create conditions in agreement with it, and it can do that by allowing the society to freely operate. Once society, taking advantage of these conditions attains freedom, the fertile land for the birth of civil society is prepared.

However, the civil society works not to guard a democratic State as envisaged by Gramsci. Its functions are different and multiple as well. First, it tries to detect the lapses of a democratic government, brings it to public attention and may even launch agitation, asking the government to redress its wrong. It cannot, of course, force the government to mend its faults as it has no political power nor does it ever intend to join political competition, making the matter an issue. But it can surely create a strong public opinion which eventually may in a large measure determine the fate of this political competition. Second, a civil society constituted by the enlightened and well-informed representatives of the society, correctly conveys to the government the views of the society and also the latter's views on and reactions to the decisions and policies of government. Third, the government may sometimes feel the necessity of ascertaining the opinion of the people, in general, on a particular issue. Of course, members of the legislature as people's representatives are there to rely on in this matter. But the information they furnish may usually be politically biased. It is here that the government may seek the help of civil society. Since the civil society has no political colour or ambition and also no particular interest to serve it can, without any bias, communicate to the government the opinion and reaction of the people.

A civil society indeed serves as a touchstone of the strength and viability of democracy. A State that hinders the growth of civil society is obviously not a democratic State. On the other hand, in the event of civil society being very weak or virtually non-existent, democracy rather limps along or sometimes becomes a casualty, paving the way for the arrival of autocratic forces. This is exactly what happened in Pakistan for many years in the past. From the very beginning, democracy there used to be short-lived, frequently succumbing to military rule. This was mostly due to the absence of an enlightened middle class playing an active role in the formation of a stable civil society. Even today, democracy in Pakistan does not seem to have a very strong foundation because its civil society is yet to become powerful and viable. On the other hand, Bangladesh initially under the grip of army rule has now been able to dispense with this autocratic rule and install a fairly strong democratic system, wiping out to a large extent the so-called fundamentalism alien to democracy mainly because a strong civil society is now at work there.

Although to enable a civil society to stand on its own feet, an enlightened middle class is a vital necessity; the media, both print and electronic, has an important role to play in making a civil society effective. In fact, the media today is regarded as a very powerful organ of the civil society to enable the latter to assert itself against political actors and to have its voice distinctly heard by others. But in order that the media may play this useful role, it ought to be as much politically neutral as the civil society itself. If on the contrary it takes political sides, it then not only becomes an ineffective agency of civil society but also may frustrate the latter's purposes and functions.

The Marxists, including Marx himself and Gramsci, held the view that any discussion on the nature and functions of the State is incomplete without an understanding of civil society. The liberals may dispute the validity of their theories but surely they cannot dismiss the tenability of this view. Indeed the worth and effectiveness of a modern democratic State or, shall we say, a democratic government depend much on whether a civil society is well nursed and whether it, independent of politics and the political system, is constantly on the watch to ensure that the power is on the right track.

5 CHAPTER

Power

Notes

INTRODUCTION

Lexicographically, power is almost synonymous with strength. But in the study of politics, power is treated as much different from strength and not without reason. Strength may be physical or mental or both. Sometimes, an individual needs no effort to develop his strength, for by nature he may be physically or mentally strong. This is due to his physiological trait. Sometimes, though born weak in body and 'mind', he develops his mental and physical strength by tireless effort. In any case, strength is characteristically personal having no social dimension. That is, it develops at the level of the individual and has generally no relation with others. Power, on the other hand, does not spontaneously grow. That is, it is not born but acquired. One has to give efforts to earn it. Second, power is not personal but social, in the sense that unless exercised against others it makes no sense. That is, the power of a person or a group is always in relation to others. Otherwise it is strength and not power. Thus, power is by nature relational. An individual abstracted from others cannot be expected to be powerful, in a lone orbit he has no power.

Power is usually viewed as political. Taking cue from Machiavelli and Hobbes, it is treated as a capacity monopolized by the State or the government. But actually, power is not merely political but social as well. It is held, enjoyed and exercised not only by political actors but also by social actors such as a prominent social leader or social reformer, a capable businessman and an outstanding

Notes

teacher of a university, college or school. Again, power operates also within a family, a club or a social association and the like. Thus, the framework of power is very wide. However, this framework is the widest in the case of political power, for the State or the government exercises power over all persons living under it. On the other hand, a family head wields power against only the members of the family or one who is in charge of controlling the affairs of a club exercises power only against the members of the club concerned. Thus, political power is much wider in range than social power. Again, political power unlike social power can go to any extent, for it involves the power to punish an individual, imprison him and even to give the latter death sentence. Hence, political power by any measure is much greater than social power. Yet what cannot be denied is the reality that social power is operative side by side with political power.

Any discourse on power cannot avoid two basic questions: (a) What is power and what is its nature? (b) What is the source of power? The answer to the first question is that power is essentially a capacity. But the distinctiveness of this capacity is that it is an ability of the power holder to get someone take a course of action which the latter, unless under the aegis of this capacity, would not have taken. That is, by exercising power one is able to change another's position hitherto held. This change of position may be accomplished in two ways—either by persuasion or by persecution. Persuasion is mostly a means in the case of social power, for none of the social organizations and institutions has at its hand any coercive instrument to force someone to do something which otherwise he would not have done. Thus, barring exceptions, a family head or the head of any social organization always tries to change the stand or position of members under his ambit by taking to persuasion. On the other hand, the holder of political power, that is, the State or for that matter the government monopolizes the possession of coercive instruments by means of which it can compel anyone to do whatever he on his own would not like to do. Thus, we may define power as one's capacity to alter other's behaviour, attitude and position in the way the former likes by means of coercion or persuasion. However, in any case, it is a phenomenon to be found in both social and political sectors.

Coming now to the second question, it may be said as regards social power that its sources are multiple. Sometimes wealth may be the source of power. Thus, a very wealthy person by means of his wealth may establish himself as a powerful person in society. Again, an outstanding talent in any sphere may enable a person to be a powerful person. On the other hand, an extraordinary skill may sometimes be a source of social power. Further, power itself may be a source of social power. A person recognized as very powerful in society may use the power already in his possession to be more powerful in society. The source of political power, however, is different from that of social power. The ability to assert power on the part of the State is rooted in its exclusive right to use its coercive instrument. Hence, coercion is mainly the source of political power. But the question that is

Notes

related to apply coercion is: Why the State and not others is entitled to use coercive instruments? The answer is that the State alone is recognized as holding the supreme power derived from the constitution and the laws. Thus, the source of political power of the State in the ultimate analysis lies in the constitution and the laws. It is the latter that arms the State with coercive power.

Coercion, however, may assume various forms such as force, domination and manipulation. Applying force implies physical activity. That is, it involves employment of visible resources directly. Domination is different from force. Although popularly regarded as associated with force, actually it does not necessarily involve force. In fact, the fear of the power addressee about the force to be applied by the power holder usually enables the latter to establish its domination. On the other hand, force or fear of force is not an element in manipulation. It is an attempt to sway other's position by cleverly reorganizing or reorienting the realities around the power addressee without ever disclosing the intention to do so and with the political actor taking care to remain behind the scene.

Man has a natural proclivity to seek power. However, to what extent he will be successful in this power seeking depends entirely on his will and capability to acquire power. All power seekers therefore do not necessarily become powerful. But once power is acquired, the powerful tries to grab more power as he is aware of the contributory value of power. He knows that power can help him fulfil a great variety of ends such as fame, respect, security, affection and wealth. Hence, he who has built a power base for himself always tries to extend it. But others are equally keen on having power. Thus, one's quest for power is checked by the same of others. In other words, the powerful is overtaken by the more powerful. It may be said that power limits power. Power of course is limited in other ways. For instance, an individual's thirst for power is subjected to the limits of his physical and psychological attributes. Further, it may so happen that the situation is so complex that it demands a great skill to achieve more power, which an actor may not have because of his lack of the required skill. Again, the prevailing customs and usages may put a brake on the extension of power. For instance, the customary rules relating to religion and sex naturally keep the latter outside the scope of power.

As power is to be always viewed in the perspective of social relations, the latter naturally condition the nature and operation of power. That is, the demand for and the operation of power depend on the kind of society that serves as its background. Thus, the downtrodden of the society desperately busy in earning the means of livelihood hardly feel any urge for power. Further, the longing for power varies depending on the social setting. People living in urban and industrial society are more interested in power than those who live in rural society with agriculture as their main occupation.

Notes

POWER AND POLITICS

If acquiring power is an important issue in the theory of power, the capacity to hold power without inhibitions is more important. This is why it is seen that Machiavelli's theory of power presented in his *The Prince*, published in the early 16th century, elaborately discusses not only the means of acquiring power but also the strategy to hold it. It may be noted that some of his prescriptions are still followed by modern politicians, particularly those of the Third World countries such as India, making Machiavelli immortal.

Anyway, on scanning contemporary realities, it appears that political actors at the level of the State and some social actors in the society are able to hold power perpetually. But how? How is it possible for them to exercise power against others uninterruptedly? What strategy do they adopt? About this strategy to be adopted at the level of the State, Machiavelli initiated a theoretical discussion and presented a long list of suggestions. However, his suggestions are clearly inapplicable to a modern democratic government, hence the necessity of seriously probing into the question.

Undoubtedly, a government, whether democratic or autocratic, holds gigantic power and perpetually exercises it against people living under it. The monarchical government of the past did hardly care whether its subjects were willing to accept this power without question. In case of any of its subjects turning recalcitrant, it used to apply its instrument of coercion, sometimes to the extreme to bring the latter under the control of its power. This was the normal practice in England until the 17th-century Puritan Revolution and in France until the 18th-century French Revolution, just to cite a few examples of the West. In Eastern countries too the scenario was the same. For instance, in India for long the monarchs arbitrarily exercised their power without caring about its acceptability to the subjects. In modern times, in some countries it is found that an autocratic government rules amok with its power with no concern about citizens' approval of its mode of functioning.

A democratic government of course can hardly go this way. True, the modern democratic government is more or less an elite government. Yet it cannot afford to ignore the fact that it is after all made by the people and hence it is liable to be responsive to their will. Although it holds and exercises massive power, it is keen on getting such power agreed to by the people. In fact, a democratic government rules with confidence whenever it knows that it has got with it people's acquiescence to its power. But how is this acquiescence earned? What is the method followed by the government in this matter? This is a question that has chased political theorists for ages.

Notes

POWER AND COMPLIANCE

Although not an advocate of democracy, the ancient Greek philosopher Aristotle was the first political thinker to attempt an answer to this question. His solution however, though straight, was too simplistic. His thesis was that as man is by nature a political animal, he has no other choice than to be a member of the State. The implication of this compulsion is evident: as a political animal, man is ordained to accept the State and its power. True, Aristotle gave a try to add a moral colour to the question as he said that the purpose of the State is to secure for all the highest good, which is essentially a moral good. Thus, the individual submits to the power of the State on the basis of the consideration that it is instrumental to his moral advancement. Many hundreds of years later, T. H. Green, a 19th-century English idealist philosopher, gave almost a similar explanation. He held that as the State is contributory to the common good which happens to be the moral ideal in the life of the individual, the latter in the interest of his moral development feels obliged to accept State's exercise of power over him. Theoretically, this moral explanation sounds excellent. But in real life it seems absurd, for it is hardly a reality that whenever an individual in his daily life agrees to do whatever he is asked to do by the political power holder, he does it voluntarily and as a conscious moral being who is much concerned about his moral development.

Two social contract theorists, Hobbes and Locke, argued that the individual submits to political power because he has, by his consent, created it and also agreed to accept it. Prima facie, this is a plausible explanation. But Hobbes in course of developing his ideas on this matter made a mockery of this consent as he finally showed the State as a 'Leviathan' who rules with immense power and loves to be extremely imposing, having no liability to the individual. This may suit autocracy but not democracy at all. Unlike Hobbes, Locke initially maintained the purity of consent. But ultimately he made a mess of it, for he argued that although the original contract was based on express consent, in the later phase when someone inherits the property of his predecessor, consent for the power of the State is implicit in his inheritance. According to Locke, this implies that to inherit property one must give his consent to submit to the State power. If he does not, he cannot enjoy the inherited property. That is, he is forced to give his acquiescence, which in true sense is no acquiescence at all. Further, one may ask: What about those who have no property to inherit? Locke has no answer to this question. The first serious attempt to resolve the issue was made by Rousseau, another social contract theorist. His point is quite simple. He argues that by submitting to the State's power, the individual actually submits to himself because it is the general will that determines the State and represents his will as well. Therefore, submission to general will is in fact submission to himself. Apparently, it seems to be a very satisfactory explanation. But

Notes

unfortunately it is no practicable solution, for Rousseau completely fails to provide the tools for ascertaining the general will. Thus, Rousseau's solution is really no solution.

The 18th-century German philosopher Hegel also explored the grounds of people's acceptance of the State power, but not quite successfully. He took the State as a supreme moral institution and also as the embodiment of highest reason. Further, he held that realization of freedom of the individual consists only in reason. Naturally, according to him, in order that an individual may turn into a moral being and in order that he may attain freedom, he must place himself at the altar of political power. T. H. Green, as seen earlier, gave a moral explanation to resolve the issue. But this moral explanation being fully abstract does not stand the test of reality. Bentham, an 18th–19th-century English political thinker, worked out a very simple solution. To him the State is an institution very much necessary for the individual, for it ensures greatest happiness of the majority and since the individual, so supposes Bentham, is one among the majority, he accepts a politically powerful State as useful to his interest. That is, man is calculative and prudent about his own good which lies in his happiness and it is on this consideration that he submits to political power. But what Bentham failed to realize is that besides the majority in society, there is a minority as well which is composed of individuals no doubt. Why then the latter, it may be asked, would obey political power when the State as per Bentham is least interested in securing them good or happiness? People, after all, do not include only the majority but minority as well.

The major fault of all these political thinkers, beginning with Aristotle, is that they all looked at the issue from the perspective of the individual and not of the State. They took it for granted that the power holder hardly needs any effort to get itself accepted by the citizens because the latter willingly consider it as their duty to extend their loyalty to political power. In view of this, the only task for them they felt was to find out the reasons behind the citizens' deeming it as their duty to remain obedient to political power. But the issue is not as simple as that. Citizens' loyalty cannot be spontaneous. Further, it is not uniform and stable. Its degree also varies. Therefore, what is required is an earnest effort on the part of the power holder to get itself uniformly and perpetually obeyed. This is possible only when he who holds power and exercises it earns a right to have this power and exercise it.

SOURCE OF POWER

But how is that possible? In the mediaeval period of Europe, it was easy to answer this question, for it could be argued then that the holder of political power got from God as his agent his absolute right to exercise power over others. As this kind of argument is simply obsolete in modern times, one has to look to other directions for a satisfactory answer. To start with, it may be said that since a democratic government works on the basis of periodic elections, it earns the right to power through the process of elections. In fact, the noted social scientist Talcott Parsons is of this opinion. There is indeed no doubt about the fact that elections add to a government's legality but surely not popularity, without which it is not possible for the government or, for that matter, for the leader of the government to extend its influence and power beyond the periphery of law. Or it may be said that a government may win greater confidence and support of the people by continuous official propaganda, true or false, at the cost of squandering the public exchequer. But the result may be only temporary because people may initially believe what is disseminated through propaganda. But whenever this propaganda goes on endlessly, people get tired of it and may eventually begin to doubt the veracity of this propaganda. Again, a government may patronize a select group of individuals, lavishly distributing rewards among them, and the latter like Gramsci's traditional intellectuals, blow trumpets in favour of the government ('a practice highly popular to the recent governments of West Bengal, a state of India). But people generally are not so foolish as to instantly accept their credibility because they know that this group, unlike Gramsci's organic intellectuals, does not work independently but only as so-called agents of government.

To resolve the issue, ideology may be brought into consideration. It may be said that a government may inculcate among the people a particular ideology so much so that the latter, constantly tutored in that ideology, may view the government as a true embodiment of the ideology they have been indoctrinated with. But the truth is that the power holder's right emanating from ideology is found to be fragile. This has been well proved by the collapse of the socialist system in the Soviet Union and the Eastern European countries. The proposition may be objected to by citing the example of China. It may be said that Chinese socialist system has been running uninterrupted all these years and to this socialist ideology has a great contribution. However, the fact is that with the introduction of market economy, ideology has completely evaporated from the Chinese system. China is now a socialist country only by name and not in fact.

In democracy, ideology is rarely found to be playing any role. However, if it does, the result may be far from satisfactory. It may even be disastrous. In Britain, as long as the Labour Party functioned politically with its diehard ideology, it was left in the wilderness, far away from power. Only when it tempered its ideology and began like a party befitting parliamentary democracy, it won credibility from the people and was able to occupy the seat of power. A similar experience is found in the state of West Bengal of India. As long as the Marxist party rigidly clung to its ideology, it could not achieve stable rule. Only after it

Notes

had compromised its ideology in favour of a parliamentary system, it was able to continue a stable government for a long period.

POWER AND AUTHORITY

Actually, when a power holder achieves a decisive right to his exercise of power, he earns authority which presupposes recognition by others of the power holder's right to power. Hence, a power holder is entitled to hold and exercise power only when his power gets transformed into authority. But how does this transformation take place? This is where Max Weber, the German sociologist, is of relevance. According to him, power undergoes this change through the process of legitimation. To put it simply, power when legitimized becomes authority. Obviously, there is much difference between power and authority. One may have power, but no authority. Again, one having authority may have little power. For instance, the head of a caretaker government in India has power but very little authority. On the other hand, a very weak prime minister like the British Prime Minister Alec Douglas-Home, who succeeded Harold Macmillan, enjoyed authority but not much power.

What then is legitimacy and how is it acquired? It may be defined following S. M. Lipset as the capacity of the power holder to generate trust among the people that the system he runs and his power are meant to do good to them. As regards the methods or means to earn this legitimacy, political scientists generally make use of Max Weber's conceptualization. According to him, there are three sources of authority, or to put it differently three ways of earning legitimacy, which are tradition, charisma and formal office (which he names as rational-legal source). To spell out, he says that the power holder may try to have legitimacy by means of long-standing tradition prevailing in the society. Or he may earn legitimacy by means of charisma, that is, by capitalizing his extraordinary personal qualities that easily attract the people.

Again, the rational-legal source may be utilized, that is, he may earn legitimacy depending on the glow of the lofty office he holds, sanctioned by ordinary law or the constitution.

Weber's typology may of course be supported by facts. For instance, the British democratic political system is traditionally wedded to the system of monarchy. Hence, though the British queen is absolutely without any real power, she enjoys from the people great respect and hence authority by way of the traditional practice in Britain. Some of the examples of charismatic authority are Mahatma Gandhi, Jawaharlal Nehru and Indira Gandhi. Mahatma Gandhi detested having any political power; at a certain stage of his political career, he

Notes

was not even a member of the Congress party. Yet because of his sterling human qualities he was able to establish his firm authority among the people of India. Besides being a political leader and the prime minister of India, Jawaharlal Nehru was a person of very many outstanding qualities. So he enjoyed authority not merely as the prime minister of India but more so as a man India had rarely seen. After winning the Bangladesh War, Indira Gandhi proved herself as an outstanding leader of the country, characterized by firm will, determination and very able statesmanship, making herself dear to the people of India. Hence, at this stage she held enormous authority because of her charisma. The third source of authority according to Weber is the rational-legal source. What he means by it is that a legally constituted office itself gives authority to its incumbent who is entitled to exercise it over others. Thus, the office of the prime minister endows its occupant authority over others.

It will not be beside the point to mention that Weber, a great believer in ideal type naturally took these three types of authority as ideal types. Hence, there is reason to doubt to what extent his concepts may be put into practice. Perhaps realization of this problem led Weber to admit that in actual practice authority is a combination of the three types he specified. Yet there is much to say against the Weberian concept of legitimacy. However, Weber is right as far as rational-legal authority is concerned. A constitutional office or a statutory office definitely entails some authority. There is no doubt about it. But the point is (and this is ignored by Weber) that whether the incumbent of the office possesses the skill and capacity to assert the authority he derives from this office. As noted earlier, British Prime Minister Alec Douglas-Home's poor authority illustrates this point. Again, sometimes political compulsions make an office holder so much incapacitated that he fails to assert the authority he has derived from his office. For instance, H. D. Deve Gowda, the prime minister of the first United Front government of India, and the Indian Prime Minister I. K. Gujral, succeeding him, could not assert their authority just because they led a very weak and unstable government. Even the prime minister of the second United Progressive Alliance (UPA) government of India, Dr Manmohan Singh, was all along found to be lacking appropriate authority because of the compulsions of coalition.

There is, however, enough reason to have misgivings about Weberian tradition and charisma. In the present age, when tradition has been fast giving way to modernity there is little chance for the political power holder to make a good use of it to his advantage. Further, tradition at least in the political world may work only temporarily but it cannot be a lasting base of political authority as tradition itself, in the present context, seems to be in a continuous flux everywhere in the modern world. The case of British monarchy is just an exception. About charisma, it may be said that first, very few political power holders are born with or later develop in life outstanding personal qualities. Second, even if a power holder has charisma and utilizes it to legitimize his power, he cannot

Notes

expect that it will continue forever, for charisma is by nature fragile. Any moment it may collapse. Otherwise Indira Gandhi, the Indian prime minister with extraordinary charisma, would not have lost the elections in 1977.

The originality of Max Weber's classification of authority in terms of its sources can by no means be denied. Also, his idea of rational-legal authority cannot altogether be dismissed, as there is an element of truth in that. But tradition and charisma can hardly be taken as the veritable and dependable sources of political authority. Of course, at the social level tradition and charisma may often be a source of authority. For instance, in the backward rural society of India, dominated by the caste system, an upper-caste priest engaged in performing religious rites by tradition enjoys some authority over the low-caste downtrodden who are generally guided by the dictates of the former. Or in such society when the majority are illiterates, an educated person like a village teacher earns authority over the former. Whereas in an urban society a social reformer for his great acts of reform is often found to have charisma. Thus, tradition and charisma may be a dependable means for legitimizing social power but certainly not political power. To that extent, Weberian legitimacy holds good.

This shows that though Weber's theory of legitimacy is original and hence commendable, it is incomplete and inadequate. What then is needed is to identify a new source of authority. It may be said that this source is functional. That is, it is the performance of the power holder or the government that is the ultimate determinant of its authority. Thus, if a political leader without attending to the interests of his party, is keen on giving his entire effort to serving the public interest, he can easily legitimize his power. On the other hand, if a government performs very well in its governance keeping in view the public interest alone, it automatically enjoys greater authority over the people. If, on the contrary, it performs poorly its authority, despite flowing from the formal office, will naturally decline. In a democracy, people generally elect the power holder mainly on the basis of its promises given before the election. But once the government is installed, they constantly keep a watch on the former and judge its performance in the light of the promises given earlier. Thus, people actually are the real source of authority. At least in a democracy it is difficult to hoodwink them by invoking tradition or charisma.

6 CHAPTER

Freedom

Notes

INTRODUCTION

After John Locke, a 17th-century English political philosopher, had in his theory claimed freedom as the natural right of man, it has been one of the most discussed subjects of political theorists for ages. Freedom denotes liberation from bondage. It is a state of things where man is free to think, move and act, however, subject to restrictions. Thus, the very word freedom whenever brought under consideration immediately raises the question: Freedom from what or whom? The question evidently implies that in an isolated living man cannot enjoy his freedom. It requires other things or persons who represent the perspective for the enjoyment of his freedom. In other words, freedom definitely has a social dimension. Viewed from this angle, it appears that T. H. Green was right when he regarded that freedom by nature is social.

Although freedom was first properly conceptualized in the 17th century, man's struggle for it has a long history. In fact, it began in the early dawn of human civilization. In primitive days, when man was a wanderer in jungles and when his intelligence, knowledge and experience were too poor, making him utterly incapable of developing instruments of production, and when collective hunting was the only means of his livelihood, he was in bondage to nature. He looked at nature with awe and used to regard it as invincible. In such a situation, he reconciled himself with his lot by attributing divinity to natural forces and tamely surrendered to them as awesome. Thus, man at this stage was an unfree animal denuded of self-confidence.

Notes

However, in course of time, when man learnt the use of fire and metals were discovered by him, he could develop the instruments of production. As a result, the situation underwent a radical change. A confident man now conscious of the strength of his arms began struggling with nature in order to conquer it. The more he achieved this feat, the more he attained freedom from the fear of nature or for that matter freedom from overpowering nature. Interestingly, even after scores of centuries and despite fantastic scientific developments, man has not yet been able to have fullest freedom from nature's control. In many matters, he is still at the mercy of nature. This indeed is one of the paradoxes of human civilization.

After having been able to overcome substantially his fear about nature, man had to face a new adversary to fight against for his freedom. This was when he entered into a community based on associative living. Since community life was more or less organized, it naturally had to accept a leader, who by virtue of his superior qualities and also because he had in his possession most of the instruments of production took charge of controlling the community life. So he was immensely powerful. As a result, man's freedom was at stake. His way of life was subjected to the forbidding canons and precepts of the leader. Accordingly, man had to launch his struggle for freedom, but with little success. Again, it was really no struggle. The community leader, conscious of his strength and advantages was unrelenting in relaxing his control. Whatever concessions were granted did not come to man as a matter of right. They only came as a matter of clemency and generosity on the part of the community leader.

Eventually, the community yielded to a full-fledged society with many unwritten rules, many of which imposed control and inhibitions on the individual, which obviously affected his freedom. Sometimes this control used to be too severe, creating a situation which ages after was regarded by John Stuart Mill as social tyranny. But man had to mostly bear with it without any protest. This was due to two reasons. First, man had yet to learn how to organize to form a collectivity that alone could stand against unseemly control inimical to his freedom. Second, he along with others in the society agreeably accepted most of these controls as he realized that he ought to do it for the survival of his social life. This was the beginning of man's realization that freedom does not mean whatever one likes to do and that it needs to be tempered with control.

This social control eventually turned into political control when State, in a rudimentary form, came into being in ancient Greek society. The State in this Greek society was a city state, much different from the nation state of modern times. Yet it was very powerful and, as Aristotle with immaculate logic tried to establish, was an omnipotent State posing a threat to the freedom of the individual. True, the Greek city states like Athens embraced direct democracy. Thus, citizens of the city state could participate in the functions of the State in as far

Notes

as they were allowed to take part in the legislative process. But they represented only the minority of the society. The non-slave owning class, who were small traders, businessmen and small agriculturists, unable to compete with the slave owners, were gradually degraded to the level of what, in Marxist parlance, is called the proletariat. On the other hand, the large number of slaves who constituted the majority of the people were treated as crass machine having no right to life, let alone freedom. Thus, freedom in the ancient Greek city state was a privilege of the few.

The situation hardly changed with the emergence of the Roman state. True, the imperial Rome introduced cosmopolitanism and provided the base of modern jurisprudence. This no doubt was a significant change. But the State power with its immense military strength was highly oppressive, denying freedom to the majority of the people. Actually, the Roman state like the Greek city state was based on a society where the slave owners ruled the roost. The sacking of Rome by the Visigoths in 410 AD was followed by an interregnum, marked by a bloody period of about 60 years' uninterrupted barbarian invasion of the imperial Rome, resulting in a loss of civilization. Europe turned into a barren intellectual land.

Taking advantage of this intellectual vacuum, Christianity began spreading fast and consolidating its strength. Thus, before the end of the 8th century, a spiritual Rome replaced imperial Rome, where the Pope as the head of the Christian order began wielding his spiritual authority almost like a Roman emperor. This authority remained intact for more than 700 years. Under the influence of this authority, there grew a milieu where man was tutored to depend on God and His self-styled representative Pope to determine everything in his life. Accordingly, he learnt to treat the Church of Rome as the only organization to which he was liable to give his total subjection. Thus, human freedom was virtually buried.

EVOLUTION OF THE CONCEPT OF FREEDOM

A spectacular change in the climate of opinion, however, set in under the influence of the 15th-century European Renaissance. It brought about a mental revolution in man in that he was now able to free himself from the theological bondage that crippled his autonomy for more than 700 years. Abjuring his erstwhile practice of submitting to the fiat of God and the Pope of Rome, he now looked at himself and discovered that he was all an uninhibited being, who with his own power could explore the unknown and force miraculous changes. Thus, in the light of the Renaissance, he became aware of his freedom and achieved enough confidence to assert it. On the other hand, a secular nation state began to evolve.

Notes

With the emergence of the State, there no doubt came about a situation favourable for the formal recognition of freedom by means of the laws of the State. However, since the birth of the State it took several hundred years to give effect to formalization of freedom, for so long as sovereignty of the State laid in a person, that is, so long as the State was under the aegis of a monarch or an autocrat, people were actually without freedom as the word of the former was regarded as law, blocking the road to freedom. It was at this stage that man's struggle for freedom against the ruler really began. It was a real struggle, for man had now learnt to be organized along with others to launch a sustained movement for freedom. Further, although his immediate purpose was to wrest freedom, his final target of attack was the personal sovereign. In fact, he went on intensifying his struggle to put an end to the system of personal sovereignty, devolving sovereignty on the people.

Eventually, thanks to the Puritan Revolution and Glorious Revolution of the 17th-century England, the struggle met with success and the political system underwent a radical transformation, signalling the arrival of democracy. Democracy, based on the principle of popular sovereignty naturally created a climate congenial to the enjoyment of freedom by the individual. Since then, freedom of the individual has traditionally been regarded as one of the chief marks of democracy. No wonder in the modern world a democratic political system is found to recognize in clearest terms freedom of the individual either by its constitution or by its laws. However, this does not mean recognition of the right of an individual to do whatever he likes to do. As a social and political animal, man has a conglomerate of obligations, which he cannot disavow by means of his freedom. That is, man's freedom is subjected to restrictions imposed on him by the overriding interests of the State and society. However, such restrictions must be reasonable; that is, they must not go beyond the boundaries set by the needs of State and society. Freedom, it may be added, can flourish only in a secular environment. If religion is allowed to go beyond the private life of the individual, if the State and society fail to keep themselves away from religion, the individual in the midst of this religion-centric social and political environment falls prey to the dominance of religion and is inevitably subjected to a kind of mental and moral servitude that kills his substantive freedom. Thus, freedom cannot thrive in a non-secular social and political milieu. The point may be illustrated by citing the case of India, a recognized democratic State. India of course is not a theocratic State. In this country, there is no State religion and the State, as clearly laid down in Articles 25–28 of the Indian Constitution, has no bias for any particular religion. Yet it appears that some political power seekers in this country are ever keen on exploiting people's religious sentiments to occupy the seat of power through the electoral process. That is why one notices a facile use of religion as a marketable commodity in the Indian electoral market. Further, as the society is saturated with religion, the latter is often found to incite social conflict, threatening individual freedom.

Notes

POLITICAL FREEDOM

The interest of the political scientists, it appears, generally centres round political freedom. The democratic State also usually puts most of its focus on political freedom that mainly includes freedom to be a party to the political process and freedom to participate in political competition. This shows that political freedom essentially means freedom from political control. However, it is not absolute but limited in the sense that it does not give one the liberty to disobey the laws and orders of political authority. This is the obligation of the individual while enjoying his political freedom. But political authority, on its part too, has an obligation towards the individual while it recognizes his political freedom. Unless in an exigency, it cannot interfere with the political freedom it has granted. Further, it has an obligation in so far as it normally cannot control personal freedom of the individual as the latter constitutes the base of one's identity and personality.

Those who view freedom from a legal point of view are of the opinion that freedom is generated by ordinary laws as well as the fundamental laws of the land, that is, the constitution. By this, what is meant is that the source of freedom is laws enacted by the State or in other words political authority in the ultimate analysis is the source of freedom. But this sounds slightly anomalous as it amounts to suggesting that prior to the State or government, there was no freedom at all which is far from true. It also implies that the State gives birth to freedom, which is to be mainly used against the former, which is logically absurd. Those who view freedom from a moral standpoint argue that freedom is an institutionalization of man's moral power meant to be used for his moral development. But had it been so, then everyone living in a democratic State and enjoying a lot of freedom would have been morally developed, which is far from true. There is again the other view, mainly that of Hegel, that freedom lies in reason and as the State represents the highest embodiment of reason, the highest and largest amount of freedom results from totally surrendering to the diktat of political authority. However, to the freedom lovers it does not convey much sense as it is really an apologia for the omnipotence of the State. Again, there is the view of Rousseau that man is born free, but then he is put into chains by his surroundings, that is, by the society and the State he is born in. The first part of the proposition is absolutely correct. Man really is born free, for he is born with no inhibitions. But it is an overstatement to say that after his birth he finds himself in chains everywhere, for it cannot be empirically proved that as man grows up he begins to be subjected to control and prohibitions denying him freedom. On the contrary, what happens in fact is that after his birth man starts tasting freedom bit by bit.

Actually, the source of freedom is man himself, for, after all, he deserves freedom and not the other species of animals. He deserves freedom because he is a

Notes

self-conscious being. He is constantly conscious of himself as much different from the rest of the animals as well as the inanimate world and accordingly conscious of his responsibility not only to remain a true human being but also to make himself a better human being by means of his ideas, deeds and conduct. To fulfil this mission in his life, he feels that he needs to move and act freely. That is, he realizes that to remain a man and to strive for being a better man, the essential requirement for him is freedom. It is in this sense that man is the source of his freedom.

Since man himself is the source of freedom, and accordingly he naturally earns a right to it, he cannot afford to neglect his duties while enjoying it. First, he must use his freedom in such a way that it is worthy of a human being. That is, he must not misuse his freedom to the extent of doing whatever he likes to do. In other words, he must rest his freedom on reason and restraint so that he does not indulge in any misdeed that befits only a brute and not a human being. Second, he ought to remember that others in the society are also human beings like him, so he must exercise his freedom in a way that does not affect the freedom of others. Third, he should use his freedom as a means to develop his inherent qualities in order that he may continuously achieve self-development. He ought to keep in mind that his freedom is not for nothing, but wedded to a definite purpose and that purpose is to better himself and society as well.

INDIVIDUAL FREEDOM

There are various forms of freedom. Of them, the most important is personal freedom. This is because personal freedom means freedom of someone neither as a citizen nor in any other role in society but just as a human being, a unique species differentiated from other creatures by his self-consciousness, intelligence, reason and wisdom. As noted previously in order that he may live as a true human being with all his distinguishing characteristics kept intact, he needs certain conditions favouring the development of his manhood. These conditions together constitute his personal freedom. The history of this freedom is much longer than that of any other form of freedom. Indeed, man's struggle for freedom began with his struggle for personal freedom. In the earliest phase of human civilization when man began his struggle against the dominance of nature, it was actually his struggle for personal freedom.

Unfortunately, it appears the interest of political scientists generally centres round political freedom as against the State. They usually desist from going into the niceties of personal freedom, the most important kind of freedom. That is why an answer to the questions what is personal freedom and what it is made of is conspicuous by its absence in modern political theory. The ingredients of personal freedom have mostly been determined by modern judicial

Notes

decisions in countries such as the USA and India, where judiciary is empowered to interpret the constitution. But strangely enough, even judicial decisions have scarcely noted that in the modern world, the most important aspect of personal freedom is freedom of choice. It is generally accepted that in the democratic political system, citizens must have a right to freely exercise their freedom of political choice, for otherwise a democratic government will hardly be a popularly elected government and as a result democracy will turn into a farce. In advanced democracies of the West, people of course enjoy fullest freedom of political choice and so democracy there runs with shining success. But unfortunately in Third World countries such as India, the scenario is much different. Here, use of money power, muscle power and various other unfair means forces the people to make their political choice in the way they are directed. As a result, people are denied their right to exercise their freedom of political choice.

But man is not only a political entity participating in the political process but also an economic entity playing principally the role of a consumer. However, if society is to be truly a democratic society, man must have full freedom of choice as a consumer and as a buyer. That is, free from all control and influence he alone should be able to decide which one to buy in the market and which one not to. Unfortunately, in recent times in view of total commercialization both in the developed and developing countries, man as a buyer of goods has virtually lost his freedom of choice. There is nothing wrong in the practice that a manufacturer will try to sell his goods by means of advertisement, the purpose of which is to inform the buyer that the product concerned is available for sale in the market and that truly it has some qualities that distinguish it from other similar products offered for sale. But with the wide use of electronic media throughout the world in recent times, the concept of advertisement and its mode as well have undergone phenomenal changes much to the detriment of a buyer's freedom of choice. For instance, many of the commercial advertisements, it is found, contain pack of lies or false information just to convey a message to the buyers that the product in question is the best among similar products available. Further, through the electronic media, the advertisement concerned is telecast again and again, sometimes four or five times in a few minutes' commercial break, in order to put pressure on the brain of the viewer and confuse his power of judgement so much so that the viewer, without thinking, further rushes to buy and then uses the product advertised. This means that in the context of modern phenomenon of commercialization, man as a buyer and as a consumer has largely been denied his freedom of choice. Needless to say, this loss of freedom of choice is tantamount to loss of personal freedom. A democracy that duly grants political freedom and other forms of freedom but fails to ensure personal freedom, particularly freedom of choice, must be regarded as incomplete. Hence, it may rightly be said that loss of freedom of choice of the individual has brought in a crisis of identity for democracy.

Notes

POSSIBILITY OF FREEDOM

Among all the liberal thinkers who have dwelt on freedom, one finds a common tendency to avoid a very crucial question: Is freedom possible? They have all argued in favour of freedom, produced long tracts on its essence and form, but never doubted its possibility as they have taken it for granted that since man is superior to all other animals, the possibility of his being free lies in his superiority in this respect. But they have furnished no criterion for objectively testing this hypothesis. Freedom, after all, does not come to man automatically. It is a result of man's struggle. As noted at the very start, man's first struggle for freedom began against nature. Of course, man was successful in this struggle but not fully. The struggle is still going on, for even in the 21st century there are many things of nature yet unknown to man and many of it yet unconquered. This shows that man is yet subject to the laws and whims of nature. For instance, with the aid of highly improved technology, he can at best forecast impending natural calamities, but cannot prevent or control it. Further, many of the mysteries of nature remain unresolved by man. Thus, at least in relation to nature, man is not fully free.

Again, in the traditional agriculture-oriented societies of backward nations, irrational superstitions, age-old beliefs, traditional caste considerations and the like still die hard. These are all an affront to the freedom of man. Yet many are found to act on them and many others are forced to surrender to them. In both cases, freedom remains beyond the reach of man. Even in the developed countries of the West, superstition and faith, rites and rituals are found to persist in the society which otherwise is highly urbanized and modernized. This signifies a society where man's freedom inevitably becomes a casualty.

It may be pointed out that freedom of man, we have so far discussed and of course brought to the focus by most of the political thinkers, is external freedom, that is, it is freedom from the control of State and society, freedom from the material world and the like. In other words, it is objective freedom. But freedom is subjective as well. This subjective freedom is man's freedom from self which is located in man's mental world. This mental world is a very complex domain comprising both good and bad, both virtue and vice. To elaborate, man's mind has both rational and irrational parts. The rational part contains his good wishes, his inclination to do good to others, to help and assist them when they are in distress and to refrain from harming them. The irrational part, on the other hand, represents his evil nature to commit offences, to envy and usurp others' property and to be led by unbecoming lust and passion. To be a true human being deserving freedom, man has first to get over these mean propensities. In other words, as charity begins at home, man's struggle for freedom must first begin within himself and his only instrument in this battle is his reason. Unless with the aid of reason, man is able to lighten this dark area of the mind. That is,

Notes

unless he is rational enough to win over his evil nature in order to prove himself a true human being far superior to other animals, he does not deserve freedom nor can he claim it, for as has been noted at the very start of this piece, only man deserves freedom just because he is a human being quite different from the rest of the animals.

This leads one to the conclusion that freedom is possible when man is not just externally free but also internally free, when his internal world glows with the light of reason. Viewed from this angle, reason is the ultimate source of freedom. Hence, it may be said that although Hegel equated freedom with reason with the ultimate purpose of legitimizing the omnipotence of the State, in a sense he was right, for nobody can deny that reason in the final analysis, is the root of freedom.

7

CHAPTER

Equality

INTRODUCTION

Notes

Man's sense of equality developed much later than that of freedom. As noted earlier, in primitive times man began fighting with nature for his freedom, but completely unaware of the necessity of equality in his life. Later, when society and State evolved in succession, he was concerned about his freedom but not about equality. The same is found at the level of ideas. Political theory went on for long without a theory of equality. Even when the liberal theory of the State took a definite shape, outlining the principle and structure of democracy, the emphasis clearly was on freedom and not on equality. It was only when the Industrial Revolution laid bare the wide disparity between the rich and the poor in the 19th-century England, justifying Disraeli's theory of 'two nations' that theorists began to give their attention to the problem of ensuring equality. Thus, Karl Marx, the historic apostle of human equality, elaborately developed a theory to probe the root of inequality and prescribed measures to put an end to it. On the other hand, John Stuart Mill, a 19th-century liberal thinker, and English socialists in their own way tried to explore ways and means for eradicating the curse of inequality. The 20th-century liberals, particularly Harold Laski, went along the same path. As a result, today most of the political scientists treat equality as an important issue of politics.

Men actually are born unequal and as they grow up, their inequality augments. Between two newborn babies, there may sometimes be close similarity

Notes

except in respect of gender and racial features. But similarity does not mean equality, for among these two babies, there may be great differences. Thus, one may be reared up in affluence, while the other in abject poverty. Further, this similarity does not last long. Everywhere in the world, adults are found so different from each other. They are different in height and weight, physique and complexion, intelligence and skill and so on. Thus, men are ordained by nature to be unequal. Viewed from this angle, it may be said that inequality is one of the stark realities of our life. Yet the demand for equality has been going on for several hundreds of years with yet no final solution to the problem.

One may however raise the question why equality is necessary for man. There have been varied answers to this question. Rousseau, an 18th-century philosopher, it may be noted, was the first modern thinker to make the strongest plea for equality. He regarded inequality in society as unnatural and unfair, and further held the view that human civilization would be at stake in the absence of equality. However, he felt no qualm about the natural differences among human beings and agreed that some kind of inequality resulting from rewarding a person for his outstanding contribution to society is permissible. On the other hand, Bernard Mandeville, Immanuel Kant and David Hume were of the opinion that by making a good use of freedom some become worthier than others. But in the name of equality, the more worthy are put at par with the less worthy, and hence equality is opposed to freedom. According to Acton, freedom presupposes an essential condition for the natural development of a man's personality, but equality arrests this natural development. All these thinkers undermining equality were, of course, liberals and that shows that liberalism generally prioritizes freedom over equality. Even Barker, a 20th-century liberal thinker, seems to be led by his conviction that freedom matters more than equality.

However, some of the 20th-century liberal theorists led by Harold Laski held a positive view about equality. Laski forcefully argued that democracy is impossible without equality, and as freedom may be realized only within the democratic framework freedom naturally thrives in a situation where equality prevails. The strongest defence in favour of equality however has come from the Marxists of course on an altogether different consideration. To them, equality is far more important than freedom, as they argue that freedom of man is impossible without equality. By this equality they mean economic equality. According to them, so long as the means of production are under private ownership, society would remain a class-divided society, and in this society, the owning class is the ruling class having absolute dominance over others, frustrating any possibility of economic equality. But without this economic equality, man can hardly enjoy freedom. Hence, what is necessary is socialization of the means of production abolishing private ownership of the means of production and it is only then that

Notes

economic inequality will come to an end, ensuring freedom of the individual. The Marxist approach is no doubt innovative. But the trouble is that nowhere in the world, not even in the countries which effected revolution with the promise of effacing private ownership of the means of production, economic equality in the Marxist sense is found to have been achieved.

This failure of the Marxist theory naturally leads one to turn to the liberal theory of equality. Fortunately, modern liberal theorists it seems have abjured the older ideas on the question. Taking cue from Laski, they now hold that liberty and equality are not at all in conflict but are complementary to each other. So they think that both liberty and equality are equally important for man. If all men living in a society are equally denied freedom, they of course enjoy a kind of equality. But in such a life without any freedom equality makes no sense. On the other hand, if some men are given freedom with others deprived of it, then in the absence of equality it will surely augur ill, for those enjoying freedom will unnecessarily and of course without right will dominate over those bereft of freedom. Thus, both equality and freedom are necessary for man. As freedom is impossible without equality, freedom is a veritable road to equality.

TYPES OF EQUALITY

Equality may be of various kinds like natural equality, that is, equality derived from the world of nature, religious equality, political equality, legal equality, social equality and so on. The Stoic philosophers of ancient Greece, who emerged after Greece had lost its independence to Rome, were the first propagators of natural equality. Watching the world of nature, they discovered that the laws of nature were equally applicable to all, irrespective of whether one was rich or poor, male or female, literate or illiterate, honest or dishonest and intelligent or stupid. This is how the Stoics engendered the idea of what may be called natural equality.

Religious equality was a product of mediaeval Europe. During the Middle Ages, the Church of Rome managed to spread the myth in the Christian Europe that all its inhabitants with their Christian faith were brethren living under the aegis of the Church. Thus, as Christians they were all equal. At least that was the claim of the Church with the ultimate purpose of keeping the entire Christian Europe under its command. This was, it may be said, religious equality. But neither the idea of natural equality nor that of religious equality lasted long. At least in the modern world both of them have become meaningless, for modern man does not need to look into nature in order to be aware of the possibility of equality. As a rational and conscious man taking a good account of the realities of life, he knows well that equality is good for him and the society he lives in.

Notes

On the other hand, the world today is dominated by various religions, not alone by Christianity. Thus, the days of hegemony of the Christian order are now over. As a result, religious equality has now completely lost its relevance.

All democratic political systems in the modern world recognize political equality as one of the basic rights of the individual. The case of India may be cited as an example. In India, all citizens enjoy equality in political participation. Thus, they all enjoy the right to vote irrespective of caste, creed, education, gender and religion. Further, they enjoy equality in political recruitment. Anyone of the Indian citizens, no matter whether he is rich or poor, educated or uneducated, male or female, Hindu or Muslim or Christian or Sikh or Jain, may be a party leader, a legislator, a member of government and even may occupy the uppermost echelon of government.

Legal equality is much simpler and more concrete in form than the other forms of equality. It means that all citizens of a political society are subject to the same law, while the latter will make no discrimination, giving privilege to none, and give equal treatment and equal opportunity to all. As far as India is concerned, Article 14 of the Indian Constitution guarantees equality before law and equal protection of law and further Article 15 prohibits discrimination barring the marginal sections of people including women, children and socially and educationally backward classes of people. This discrimination in favour of the marginal people is no denial of equality and fully justifiable, as it is in the interest of social justice, as pointed out by modern political thinkers such as John Rawls and others.

Political and legal equality however do not ensure social equality. In fact, no law can establish social equality and this is why it is more difficult to achieve. As seen earlier, Marxists are of the opinion that social equality is not possible without economic equality. But as already discussed, the Marxist theory of economic equality is only theoretical, having no practical value as there is so far no evidence in the world proving that it can come into effect. On the other hand, modern liberals, less dogmatic than the earlier ones, do not believe that pursuit of a solution to the problem of equality is fruitless like going against the stream, à la Rousseau. As far as social equality is concerned, they emphasize that a free society alone may ensure social equality. There is quite a point in this argument. If a society is free, not only in the sense of being autonomous in its own sphere but also in the sense that individuals living in the society are all free from any subjection to each other, then equality automatically prevails in that society. But a free society is difficult to achieve, for in a society particularly in a country like India there are too many prejudices, taboos, and religious and economic disparities, each obstructing the healthy growth of a free society. Does it mean then that free society is not possible and so is social equality?

Notes

SOCIAL EQUALITY

At this point, it is apt to note that the above-noted hindrances against the growth of a free society are all man's creation. After all, the superstitions, prejudices and social attitudes do not drop from the sky. They are created and spread among others by man's deliberate efforts. Therefore, notwithstanding differences in physique, appearances, habits and culture among human beings, social equality is possible if all agree to make effort towards that direction, suitably reorienting their mentality, attitude and culture. But to know more about it, one must know what exactly is meant by social equality. In other words, definition of social equality is the first step in the process of finding a solution to the problem of social equality.

The given fact of a society is that human beings are far from identical, characterized by very many natural differences among them. While defining social equality, one cannot afford to ignore this stark reality. If it is so, then how is equality possible? A plausible answer to this question may be that irrespective of whatever differences there are among people belonging to a society, they may be treated equally. Thus, it may be said that social equality lies in equal treatment. However, this equal treatment, as Laski rightly pointed out, does not mean identity of treatment. That is, it does not mean ignoring differences of various kinds among people. It only means that no matter whatever be the differences among men, society must extend to them same respect, dignity, and status and rights. Needless to add, whatever is true of social equality is also true of equality in general. Thus, equality may be defined as a state of things where, accepting natural inequality of men, all are equally treated and given equal opportunity.

SOCIAL EQUALITY: THE CASE OF INDIA

In a society more or less traditional like that of India, it is, no doubt, difficult to achieve social equality. In India, the upper-caste people usually look down on the people belonging to lower castes. They consider themselves as superiors and the lower castes as inferiors. A social arrangement, clubbing them together with the lower castes, is intolerable and also incredible to them. Again, some of the lower castes are untouchables to them; they are rather a deserted herd having no right to intermix with the former despite a constitutional provision abolishing untouchability and an Indian law meant to give punishment for indulging in the practice of untouchability. Similarly, there is a wide gap between the rich and the poor, and between the educated and the uneducated. Everywhere in India, the rich and the educated enjoy a higher status. They get special treatment from the society and even from local and official administration.

Notes

In the developed societies of the West, the story is altogether different. There the high-ups and lowlies generally get almost equal treatment. This has been possible because Western societies are predominantly urban and hence modernized societies are relatively free from false beliefs, superstitions and social inhibitions. Further, the evil of caste system is completely absent there. Of course, sometimes, racial prejudices show their ugly face. But only those who lack civility indulge in such prejudices and the majority of people are free from it. In other words, in the societies of advanced Western nations, racial prejudices are not a general rule, but an exception.

It has been pointed out earlier that it is possible for the State to give equal treatment to all by means of its laws. The only condition is that such laws must be appropriate for the purpose. Similarly, social equality is possible provided that the society is sufficiently modernized to generate the appropriate social milieu. Thus, equality may be said to be directly related to modernization. The modernization however should not merely be structural. That is, mere industrialization leading to structural change of society is not enough. What is needed is a mental metamorphosis of the people. That is, equal treatment of people is possible in a society only when each one of the society, whether educated or uneducated, cultivates a rational mind. Indeed, if man is rational enough, he may realize well that whatever be the differences in respect of wealth, education, caste or religion, everyone is primarily a human being and on that score he deserves treatment equal to what is meted out to others.

To some, this may sound a too idealistic version. They may argue that it may be possible in the advanced Western societies, but in a society like that of India with rigid social hierarchy, this is hardly possible. They have a point, no doubt. In the West after all there is no inflexible social hierarchy. This is due to several reasons. First, in the West there is no caste system acting as a brake on social mobility. Second, in view of dignity and high value of labour, there is no unusual difference between mental and manual labour. Third, barring the cases of extraordinarily rich among the people in general there is no large disparity in income as a minimum economic standard is guaranteed to all. Last, sometimes a labourer engaged in a very hazardous or a risky job draws a salary higher than what is drawn by a firm manager or a university professor.

In a country like India, the given situation is altogether different. A large number of people in India lie below the poverty line. The caste system encouraging social inequality looms large in the body of society. Superstitions still die hard, leading to the growth of very many social evils. Further, dignity of labour is conspicuous by its absence. In such a situation how to establish social equality? Some noted observers of society and politics in India believe that a rapid spread of education is the only answer to the problem. But this is only an oversimplified solution, for whatever institutional education has so far been developed in India

Notes

seems to have no salutary effect on eradication of inequality. On the contrary, it generally appears that the more the people are educated, the more they look down on those who are at the lower stratum. It is even noticed that when someone belonging to a low caste or a poor family somehow overcoming adversities becomes highly educated and well placed in life, he usually alienates himself from his own family and considers himself suddenly elevated to the higher caste and class or desperately tries for this upward mobility. In other words, what M. N. Srinivas has regarded as the process of Sanskritization is found to be very much at work in such cases.

Actually, what is needed is social education permeating all levels of society and striking hard at the superiority complex of the high-ups and the endemic sense of inferiority of the downtrodden so that it may work as a social leveller. For this social education, aimed at bringing an attitudinal and cultural change of the people, what is called for is a sustained social movement and a powerful social leadership to launch and untiringly continue this movement. In the 19th-century India, the process was first set in motion by Ram Mohan Roy and then continued by other well-meaning luminaries. In the 20th-century India, the thread was picked up by Gandhi. But sadly enough, with his mortal departure the movement lost its edge.

However, no social education by way of social movement is possible unless the society itself is free from political control. In the developed countries of the West, social equality in the form of equal treatment to all has been possible to a great extent because the society is free from political interference. The State there is preoccupied with political activities, never extending its arms to the orbit of social activities. Hence, the society in these countries moves and works on its own. In British India, the foreign masters were of course aggressive and oppressive as well towards the Indian subjects. But as regards social activities, they were far from officious. In fact, this is the reason that explains why the 19th-century India could have historic social galaxies like Ram Mohan and others, and why a good many social movements could achieve success. Unfortunately, in independent India, particularly since the 1970s, the trend started on the part of the State to politicize gradually the society and today the process is complete with the result that politics has totally usurped the freedom of society. No wonder in India today social equality has been a casualty. Thus, people of India, thanks to the Constitution of India, enjoy political and legal equality but social equality unfortunately ever eludes them.

But political and legal equality without social equality make no sense. To illustrate, one may take the case of an untouchable in India. He may have the equal right of voting along with those who belong to the upper castes and classes. Further, law may not make any discrimination between him and the latter. He may avail of law in the same way as in case of others. But as a human being, he

Notes

deserves due dignity which neither political equality nor legal equality can ensure. This means that the State has no role to play in establishing social equality for all who live in society. It is the society which must take the entire responsibility for securing it to its members. As noted above, there must be for this a continuing social movement under the aegis of powerful and caring social leadership. It has already been pointed out that this social movement should aim at a fundamental attitudinal change of the people. But the question is: Where to start this movement?

The answer is that it should begin first at the level of family, as family undoubtedly represents the core of a society. As a child grows up within a family, his parents should try to transfuse in his mind the idea that no matter whatever be the differences among the members of society they should all be treated as equal, deserving equal respect and reverence from him. Inside the family too there must be an atmosphere congenial to equality among all the members of the family. That is, parents should take care that they do not make any discrimination among the little ones of the family. Whenever the children get a little mature, that is when they reach the age of making friends with others, the parents should see to it that they mix with friends on equal terms in the sense that they make friends irrespective of whether the friends are of low or high castes, rich or poor and of low or high origin. That is, parents should carefully groom their children not to be choosy about making friends or to make friends with those alone who happen to be of the same status as theirs. The child's first outlet from family takes him straight to school. Therefore, the school is no less important than the family to socialize a child in matters relating to equal treatment. Accordingly, the syllabus framers of school education should frame the syllabus in such a way and teachers ought to handle syllabus in such a skilful manner that students are able to develop an orientation in the direction of equal treatment.

Further, there must be appropriate change in social relations. There should be in it complete mobility without any inhibition. It is certainly not possible for the laws of the State to ensure this state of affairs in social relations. As an example, it may be noted that the Constitution of India forbids untouchability and there is also a law to curb the dowry system. Yet these practices go on unabated in Indian society. Further, there are many areas in India where rigid caste considerations completely obstruct mobility in social relations. This is where a large-scale social movement is needed under towering personalities like Gandhi. Unfortunately in India, because of pervasive politics having its unwholesome presence in every segment of society, society has little freedom. As a result, there is no scope for any meaningful social movement nor the emergence of social leadership. This leads one to the conclusion that in India or, for that matter, in any country where society is denied autonomy, social equality will continue to be beyond reach.

8 CHAPTER

Rights

INTRODUCTION

Notes

Man, and not other animals, has a natural claim to rights. This is so on two grounds. First, other animals are primarily engaged in three kinds of activities relating to food, shelter and sex. But human activities cover a vast area because man with his intelligence and creative talent tends to explore continuously new fields of activities, and to establish that these activities are his and not of others he needs an exclusive recognition of his capacity for manifold activities. Rights are the only means to give him this recognition. Second, an individual is always keen on asserting his identity amid the diversities around. Rights actually are a mark of this identity. To put it differently, rights are integrally related to the self of man. Thus, rights may be defined as conditions necessary for enabling a man's self-expression and also for facilitating his creative activities. Viewed from this angle, rights may be regarded as essential for the progress of human civilization.

Although rights are thus a vital necessity for man and his civilization, it took him long to understand its value and put a claim to it. In fact before the European Renaissance, one finds little evidence of awareness of it. It was only after the Renaissance when man became aware of his distinctive personality and strength that he slowly began learning the importance of rights. Thus, the first demand for rights sparked off on 31 October 1517, when Martin Luther stormed the then Christian world by asserting man's religious right to come out

Notes

of the high-handedness of the Church of Rome. Then came the Puritan Revolution setting the background for the development of rights of man in the context of which emerged John Milton with his *Areopagitica*, where he thundered about the right 'to know, to utter and to argue freely'.

At the theoretical level however the first attempt was made by John Locke, a philosopher of the 17th-century England, to theorize the rights of man. True, he made use of the social contract model in order to establish that prior to the birth of society and State, man inhabiting the 'state of nature' used to enjoy three rights—the right to life, liberty and property—and the State after it had come into being was obliged not to interfere with these rights and also to protect them. These rights came to be known as natural rights in the sense of being derived from an imaginary state of nature and long after were subjected to fierce criticism by Jeremy Bentham. But Locke's 'state of nature' was actually a part of the theoretical model he relied on for developing a theory of rights. Hence, his natural rights are natural not in the sense of being inherited from the 'state of nature' but in the sense that they are the inherent rights of man or what in modern parlance may be called human rights. Thus, Locke no doubt must be given the credit of being a pioneer in the development of the theory of rights. About a hundred years later, the French Revolution by means of the ideology guiding it put a permanent seal on the validity of the rights of man and since then rights have all along been regarded as an important subject matter of the theory of politics.

SOURCE OF RIGHTS

Finding out the source of rights is extremely important as with it is linked with the question about the nature of rights. On the source of rights, the two major theories developed up to the 19th century are legal theory and moral theory. The main exponent of the legal theory of rights was the utilitarian English philosopher Jeremy Bentham. He considers the contractarian state of nature as a mere fiction and accordingly dismisses natural rights rooted in the state of nature as utter nonsense. Had he been a little more perceptive and sympathetic to Locke, he could have well realized that instead of meaning rights originating in the fictional state of nature, what Locke implicitly meant to say was that rights are natural only in the sense that man deserves them just because they are human beings. Unfortunately, Bentham fails to take it this way because he is firm in his conviction that laws of the State are the real source of rights. True, laws of the State, both constitutional and ordinary, formally create rights of the individual. But viewed from this angle, it amounts to suggesting that conventions and customs have no role in giving birth to rights, while the fact is that in every democratic country they have more or less an important role in giving effect to rights. Further, Bentham's legal theory of rights places the individual at

Notes

the receiving end. That is, it means to say that in matters of his right, the individual is completely passive in as far as he is bound to accept docilely what is doled out by the State. This may fit in with an autocratic system, but surely goes against the very spirit of democracy. Above all, it flatly denies the historic struggle of man for his rights through ages, the struggle which is still continuing in the modern world. Thus, it may be rightly concluded that the legal theory of rights pioneered by Bentham completely belittles the importance of the individual vis-à-vis the State.

The moral theory of rights is most elaborately expounded in the writings of T. H. Green, a 19th-century English idealist philosopher. Green begins his theory by assailing, like Bentham, the theory of natural rights. Unfortunately, like Bentham, he views natural rights as derived from the contractarian state of nature. However, his criticism of natural rights leads him to a conclusion totally different from that of Bentham in that he keeps himself away from the Benthamite position that rights are the creature of laws. According to him, as a moral being, man has within himself moral power for the fulfilment of which certain external conditions are necessary and rights are nothing but these external conditions. These external conditions are provided by the State. Thus, rights are not created by the State. It only recognizes rights of man in the sense that in the ultimate analysis it recognizes the moral power of man lying within himself. Thus, to Green, the source of rights lies in the moral self of man. But it is difficult to accept the moral overtones of Green's theory of rights, for in real life, it is hardly seen that an individual while claiming his right is always conscious that he is a moral being. However, scanning Green's ideas on the issue, one finds that Green, of course, tries to meet this problem indirectly when he argues that it is the duty of man to strive for his moral development and it is in this context that man requires rights. Viewed this way, it would appear that to Green, duty enjoys greater priority than rights. Indeed, this is why Green makes his famous aphorism that rights imply duties, thereby meaning that a man, conscious of his duties, alone deserves rights. Further, remembering Green's thesis that man's moral development consists in the realization of common good or social good it becomes evident that rights are truly social, that is, man may have his rights not in isolation from others but only as a member of a society. When Green thus emphasizes the social context of rights, he is no doubt on the right track as it is true to the facts of life. The only defect of his doctrine looms large when he focuses the moral source of rights. Had he desisted from giving moral perspective to rights and simply said that rights are the conditions for the development of an individual's personality, then certainly his theory of rights could have attained tenability.

It was in the 20th century that Harold Laski presented a theory of rights free from this gross defect. Like Green, he emphasized rights as social. But he kept clear of Green's moral obsession. Again like Green, he discarded Bentham's theory of legal rights. He did not subscribe to the view that the State creates

Notes

rights. Further, he slightly modified Green's argument by saying that the State does not recognize rights; it rather maintains them. Also, he took rights as a standard for evaluating the quality of a State by arguing that the State is known by the rights it maintains. Above all, he gave the most acceptable definition of rights when he said that rights are the conditions of social life without which man cannot be himself at his best. This, it may be said, is the most agreeable definition. Although subsequently some thinkers presented different theories, Laski's approach indeed seems to be the best.

MEANINGFUL USE OF RIGHTS

Maintenance of rights of the individual by the State however is not enough to make them effective. What is required more is an environment congenial to the enjoyment of rights. In order to develop this environment, two things are necessary. The first condition is freedom and the second is equality. If man is not free to enjoy and exercise his rights, the latter inevitably turns into a stuff empty of any substantive value. That is, without freedom rights remain only a promise and hardly its fulfilment. Hence, along with maintaining the rights of the individual, it is the responsibility of the State to facilitate the development of a political process where the individual may freely exercise his rights as per his own choice. Similarly, it is the duty of the State to ensure that society freed from unnecessary political control fosters a social environment, where an individual can exercise his social rights without any hindrance. Again, the right of an individual is not his private possession to the exclusion of others. Actually, it is meant to be equally shared by all. Hence, rights to be meaningful must be coupled with equality. This shows that rights, liberty and equality are intimately related to each other. In fact, they together represent a trinity essential for the self-development of man.

An individual while enjoying and exercising his rights must take care that his rights do not interfere with the rights of others. As rights are equally meant for all, irrespective of other considerations, one's exercise of rights must not cause any impediment to that of others. In that sense, man's rights carry with them a duty to others. Hence, rights are correlative to duties and, although in a different way, that justifies Green's thesis that rights imply duties. It is interesting to note that the Constitution of India clearly acknowledges this correlation. Thus, the charter of Fundamental Rights as given by Part III of the Constitution is followed by its Part IVA, which gives a list of 11 Fundamental Duties of Indian citizens.

The two criteria vital for judging whether a political system is a democracy or not are no doubt freedom and rights of the individual. As noted earlier, freedom, both social and political, is one of the requisites of a democratic State and society. Indeed, in the absence of appropriate freedom and rights, the democratic ideal

Notes

becomes barren of any meaning. Thus, a democracy is known by the quantum and quality of freedom and rights it promotes. Rights however may be of various kinds. Of them, the most important are political rights, social rights and economic rights. The Western model of democracy on the anvil of which Indian democracy has been forged gives due importance to political and social rights but not to economic rights, as liberalism, the ideology ruling it, does not take any cognizance of economic rights. The Marxists on the other hand put primacy on economic rights and argue that this economic right may be made available to the individual only in a society where fullest economic equality prevails. But they add that this economic equality is possible only when after the proletarian revolution, the long process of planned production finally reaches a stage of abundant production where everyone gets according to his need. But there is not yet any proof in the world anywhere to substantiate that the stage of abundant production may be reached. Thus, the Marxian idea of economic rights conveys little practical meaning.

HUMAN RIGHTS

A few years after the UN had come into being, the United Nations General Assembly in 1948 adopted a document under the title *Universal Declaration of Human Rights* to provide a guideline to the member nations on the protection of human rights. Thereafter, in the 1960s two covenants were made to supplement it. Since then human rights have been in the agenda of every nation, and they obviously have come to limelight in the world. There have been various activists and organizations all over the world to look after human rights and to lodge a protest to the appropriate authority in case of violation of human rights. It should be remembered however that the term human rights is not anything new. It is the other name of natural rights first coined by John Locke, provided however, Locke's natural rights are interpreted in the way as has been done in the earlier part of this chapter.

Thus, it may be said that human rights are rights an individual deserves as a human being. But to be born as a human being and to be a member of human society is not enough to make an individual a true human being. He indeed must fulfil certain conditions. First, he must be conscious of the distinctiveness of his identity, and hence must keep in mind that in his behaviour and act he cannot afford to rule out restrictions. That is, he must be guided by reason which instructs him not to do the things which are not befitting of a human being. Second, he deserves human rights only when he is aware of his responsibility of not to disturb the public order and to respect the human rights of others. Thus, human rights are not absolute. They are subject to reasonable restrictions. This in fact is the implication of the UN's Universal Declaration of Human Rights.

It may be relevant to point out that UN's Universal Declaration of Human Rights was made in December 1948. On the other hand, the report of the Advisory Committee of the Constituent Assembly of India on Fundamental Rights was submitted and deliberated on in the third session of the Constituent Assembly that lasted up to 2 May 1947. Then, the draft Constitution of India incorporating of course the report on Fundamental Rights was made ready by February 1948. As a result, the Constitution of India had in its Part III a charter of human rights, each of which was included in the UN's Universal Declaration of Human Rights of December 1948. Thus, it may be said that the framers of the Indian Constitution forewent the UN General Assembly in matters of human rights. True, Part III of the Indian Constitution enlisting Fundamental Rights largely followed the 'Bill of Rights' of the US Constitution. But there is a difference in that the US Constitution did not originally include fundamental rights. They all were the result of subsequent constitutional amendments. On the other hand, the Indian Constitution originally incorporated Fundamental Rights. The only exception is the fundamental right of children of the age of 6–14 years to have free elementary education, a unique human right incorporated by the 86th Constitutional Amendment, 2002.

As noted earlier, rights of the individual no doubt are one of the important hallmarks of a democracy. Indeed, democracy makes no sense unless it acknowledges the value of individual rights, for democracy is based on the principle of popular sovereignty. Rights surely are one of the conditions to give effect to this ideal of popular sovereignty. Rights, recognized by modern democracy, are basically of three kinds, which are political rights, personal rights and social rights. Political right is a right to be an active participant in the political process. It includes right to vote, right to hold political power, right to compete for political power, right to form political association, right to criticize government and even to resist it. As political right ensures a political democracy, social right guarantees a democratic society which serves as the foundation of political democracy. Thus, social right is no less important than political right. It is a right to freely take part in very many social activities without any interference by the State and thus is one of the requirements to foster a free society. Personal right, on the other hand, is the right of the individual as a person. That is, it is the right of an individual to develop his personal traits which distinguishes him from others and hence helps him develop his personality in his own way, subject however to the greater interests of society. It includes the right to follow the religion of one's choice, right to perform religious rites, right to education, right to own and possess intellectual property, right to marry and divorce and so on, provided however, that the exercise of such rights does not go against the standing social norm and social ethics.

As highlighted by Locke in the 17th century, democracy recognizes the right to resist the State but not to revolution. Thus, right to resistance is an important aspect of democracy. This right implies that people living under a democratic government are entitled to resist it and replace it in case it fails to deliver the goods. But right to revolution is a right to radically alter the very social and political framework, and so it is not permissible in a democracy as it does not live with an overthrow of the existing order. As regards the right of resistance, it is pointless to debate whether the majority alone or the minority also may have the right of resistance. Actually, the right to resist the government is really a right of the individual. Thus, not just a group of individuals but even a single individual may launch and lead a movement for resistance. That indeed is the beauty of democracy.

Rights of man are of course a fruit of civilization. Hence, man has a natural claim to right. But he can put up this claim only when he is deserving of it. That is, he deserves it only when he is civilized and civil enough in his manners, act and behaviour. With his rights, he cannot do anything that is unbecoming of a man. Thus, every individual in a modern democratic State has a right to life. It is the duty of the State to respect and protect it. But whenever someone like a brute commits the most heinous offence or, to quote the judgement of the Indian Supreme Court, if someone commits a crime which is regarded as 'the rarest of the rare', the State has every right to take away permanently his most precious right to life and execute him. Viewed from this angle, it may be said MacCormick is right when he says that rights are always concerned with human goods. Similarly, although Green's theory of rights suffers from moral overtones, it cannot be denied that there is an element of truth in his implicit suggestion that man deserves rights when he has a moral sense.

Which of the rights of man is the most important among others depends on the corresponding time and social and political conditions. For instance, in earlier times, when a monarch with his personal sovereignty ruthlessly imposed his authority over his subjects, the right to be liberated from this personal rule was regarded as the most urgent. But when, in course of time democracy dawned on granting substantially freedom to the individual, the earlier urge for right to freedom much subsided. However, in the colonial countries, the right to freedom from foreign yoke became most relevant in the past two centuries. Today, in the 21st century as democracy has flourished in most of the countries of the world guaranteeing political and social freedom, the target point of rights has much changed. It is now the age of personal rights. This is due to two developments. First, because of spectacular advancement in technology man's personal life today is exposed to a very large aperture. In view of this, an individual's right to privacy is reckoned as his most important personal right. Second, in view of the fact that almost all the countries of the world have embraced a free economy, a highly competitive market has emerged. As a result, in today's commercial society, bewildering a consumer about what to choose as a buyer, the personal right to choice must be regarded as the important personal right of man.

Notes

An individual may of course exercise his rights subject however to his obligation to obey the authority of the State. The State on the other hand is under an obligation to ensure an environment where an individual is free to exercise his rights. In that sense, both the State and the individual have a duty in regard to rights. Thus, rights imply duties on the part of both the State and the individual.

9

CHAPTER

Justice

INTRODUCTION

Notes

The theoretical concept of justice is the oldest among all the ideas of the theory of politics. It evolved in ancient Greece where the State was a small city state and the society was based on a system of slavery, much different from the social and political order of modern times. Naturally, it appears rather strange that even against the backdrop of this closed system, it was possible for Plato and Aristotle—the two greats of ancient Greece—to give a hand to conceptualizing justice. Not only that, Plato also underscored a vital truth valid even today when he regarded justice as an essential virtue of the State and society. This Platonic perception is indeed the starting point of the universally agreed notion of our times that if an individual living in a society and State is denied justice, then no matter whatever amount of freedom and equality he enjoys he has just a meaningless existence, and the State and society on the other hand fail to justly deliver goods to those at the receiving end.

No wonder the modern theory of politics recognizes justice as the most important requirement in the life of the social and political man. But what then is justice? Popularly, justice is regarded as an impartial and rightful settlement of disputes between individuals and organizations. But this approach is piecemeal and hence falls far short of giving the holistic view of justice as it highlights a kind of justice which is usually known as legal justice. This legal justice is of course important, and hence in modern democratic political systems it is found

Notes

that there is an elaborate arrangement for providing legal justice to the citizens. But legal justice is just one kind of justice that is not enough to fulfil, in practice, the democratic ideal. True, modern democratic system accords another kind of justice known as political justice. Political justice presupposes granting of various forms of equality and freedom by virtue of which individuals, irrespective of caste, creed, class, religion and gender, enjoy equal rights and freedom and thereby are ensured equal status in the social and political life which no doubt is reflective of the merit of democracy as a political system.

However, justice is incomplete unless it includes social justice as well. Legal and political justice are no doubt valuable. But social justice is more valuable than them, for legal and political justice bring in a democratic atmosphere where citizens are assured of their democratic rights. Social justice, on the other hand, ensures equal dignity to all individuals not as citizens but as persons so that the latter are encouraged to develop their latent qualities as human beings. That is, legal and political justice help one be an active and effective citizen, while social justice ensures a social order where an individual gets ample opportunities to strive for the development of his personality. That is why most of the thinkers who have dwelt on the concept of justice have treated social justice as a subject of their concern.

PRE-RENAISSANCE CONCEPTUALIZATION OF SOCIAL JUSTICE

The most prominent among them is the ancient Greek philosopher Plato, who in fact initiated theoretical discussion on social justice. Its starting point is the premise that an individual's position in society is determined by the occupation he is engaged in and that in respect of this occupation, people living in society are divided into certain classes. Then, viewing justice as an essential virtue of the State, he argues that this virtue prevails only when a person permanently remains in his position and faithfully performs duties of that position as determined by the nature and functions of the occupational class to which he belongs. If the person concerned, he further argues, overrides his class position and tries to intrude into the other occupational class, social justice is in utter jeopardy. Thus, social justice propounded by Plato may be regarded as positional justice, as it is related to social position. But this positional justice indeed is no justice at all, for it presupposes an unalterable social hierarchy where there is no social mobility, where a person has no opportunity to move to the upper class by virtue of his worth and improve his social status, and where he has to tamely surrender to the status quo and accept whatever is fixed for him by his occupation. Thus, Plato's justice is clearly an outcome of the desperate urge to maintain the status quo in society. Naturally, to one who accepts the essentials of democracy it would

Notes

appear just an anachronism that hardly fits in with the spirit of modern democratic system which allows unfettered mobility by virtue of which even the poor and the lowly may go up to the highest rung of political power by means of their capability. Further, Plato's theory of justice is based on a false assumption in that it assumes that every individual is fit for one occupation and not many. This might hold good in Plato's slave society, but after the Renaissance when a modern society came into existence where a confident man began exploring very many areas of activities, man's role began to be multi-occupational and this trend continues unabated in the society of modern times. Again, the question that who allocates different positions to different occupational classes remains unanswered in Plato's theory. Thus, Plato's positional justice is inadequate, incomplete and also dangerous as it encourages an unequal order which is at odds with the idea of justice endorsed in modern democratic society. Perhaps the stagnant slave society Plato was living in and the limitations of which he could not transcend were responsible for all such failings.

Plato's successor Aristotle was also a product of slave society. However, he was able to get over to a large extent the shortcomings of his slave society as he did not propagate a closed social order. True, he could not conceive of equality as we understand it today. However, he developed a theory of proportionate equality on the basis of which he constructed his theory of justice. While doing so, Aristotle proved himself a pioneer as he viewed justice against the backdrop of distribution of rewards in a society and highlighted what in our time is regarded as distributive justice. He viewed society as an order that distributes rewards among the people and then says that a just order is that which distributes reward to a person according to his deserts, that is, according to the nature of services he renders. To put it simply, according to Aristotle under the rule of justice, one who does good work will get more than one who on that score falls behind. True, by positing proportionate equality as the basis of justice, Aristotle dismisses equal treatment, which as shown earlier forms an indispensable part of modern idea of equality, and this indeed is a lacuna of Aristotle's justice. However, with his main focus on distributive justice, Aristotle admittedly sets a trend that is found to be pursued in the modern democratic systems. Further, it appears that by his idea of justice, Aristotle does not subscribe to Plato's plea for a closed and hierarchical order. His theory of justice implicitly suggests that everybody is free to move to the higher social level, provided he can prove that he has better worth. Thus, Aristotle's justice is not as dangerous as that of Plato. In fact, this is one of the reasons why Aristotle, although a theorist of the ancient Greek city state, enjoys greater acceptability than Plato in the modern world.

Cicero, a noted philosopher of the Roman era, follows Plato in making justice the central theme of his work under the title *The Republic,* a title similar to that of the major work of Plato. Also like Plato, he believes that it is possible to develop a universal principle of justice. But when he proceeds to discuss what

Notes

justice is, he departs from Plato. He begins with the proposition that justice is to be viewed from a moral standpoint. According to him, justice is one of the four important virtues that constitute moral goodness. It is essentially generosity that leads one to treat others justly even when he himself is treated unjustly. Rejecting Plato's judgement that justice is possible in an unequal order, Cicero believes that it may be had only within the framework of natural equality. This natural equality he feels may be available only through law, the great equalizer. Thus, Cicero finally links justice to law which in his view is the right reason in agreement with nature by which, alone, it is possible to distinguish just things from unjust things. Hence, justice is dependent on law. Thus, it is seen, though Cicero's definition of law is much different from what is accepted in the modern world, he in any case views justice in the light of law. In this respect, Cicero no doubt was a pioneer. However, in the modern world Cicero's legal theory of justice hardly holds good, for law at best can give formal justice, which is no guarantee for ensuring social justice.

Further, to leave to law the sole authority to determine what is just and what is unjust is to regard political authority as the arbiter of justice, a view which for the modern democratic political system is completely untenable.

RENAISSANCE AND AFTER: THE CONCEPT OF SOCIAL JUSTICE

In the post-Renaissance period, Hobbes, a 17th-century English philosopher, was the first thinker to dwell on justice. But, by arguing that laws signify the rule determining what is just and what is unjust, he virtually reiterates Cicero and hence the same criticism against Cicero applies also to him. Further, according to him, law is the command of the sovereign. It may be said with reason that this definition of law lands him straight in the conclusion that justice, in the ultimate analysis, is what is decided by a 'leviathanic' political authority, a position that may be perfectly valid for a totalitarian system but not for democracy.

A better version was given by John Locke, a 17th-century pioneer of the liberal doctrine. Locke, of course, in his theory did not directly touch on justice. However, he gave enough indications of his approach to the question of justice in his liberal theory. Locke in this theory gave primary focus on the individual's right to life, liberty and property, which he considered as the inalienable and invaluable right of the individual. From this, it may be logically deduced that according to Locke, an individual is secured of justice whenever he gets the guarantee of protection of his right to his life, liberty and property. This is of course a very valid argument. The precondition of justice is no doubt protecting life and freedom of the individual. Indeed, right to life is essential as without it an individual's physical existence is threatened at every stage. On the other hand, if the individual is not free, if he is constantly inhibited in exercising his personal and social choice, justice will only be a mockery—so far, so good. But what is antithetic to social justice is Locke's emphasis on the right to property as an inviolable basic right, since this right, if unregulated, engenders social injustice. Thus, as regards Locke's theory of justice, it may be said that it makes a good start but ultimately falls through.

There is no doubt a promise of justice in the theory of general will propounded by Rousseau, an 18th-century philosopher. His general will to which he ascribes sovereignty is, he argues, wedded to common interest. If it is so, then certainly this general will may be regarded as a guarantee of justice, equally for all. But on closer scrutiny, it appears that while defining general will, Rousseau drowns in a morass of illusions, for he tries to show that by taking into account the pluses and minuses of the individual will, the idea of general will may be arrived at. But, unfortunately, he suggests no mechanism for working out this arithmetical sum. Thus, his theory ultimately turns out to be vague, hardly giving any hint about how to concretize general will in real life. Hence, it may be said that whatever hope of justice one initially finds in Rousseau's concept of general will finally amounts to an empty hope.

When Hume, an 18th-century English philosopher, regards justice as conducive to public good and when he further talks about justice consisting, in distribution, of material goods, he it seems is advocating a good theory of distributive justice. But when in the name of distribution he actually ascribes material goods to particular individuals with the aim of linking justice with property, his justice actually means justice not for all but only for propertied persons, and thus is discriminative justice, and hence no justice at all. Thus, Hume, almost like Rousseau, raises a false hope of justice. Bentham, an 18th–19th-century English utilitarian philosopher, like Hume, views justice completely from a different angle. However, unlike Hume, he regards laws of the State as the source of justice and thus enunciates a theory of legal justice. But his is a legal justice with a difference, for in his opinion to establish justice in the society, what the State with its laws is required to do is to secure the greatest good to the greatest number of people. Thus, Bentham apparently is in favour of distributive justice. But, actually, it is a kind of justice that is meant only for the majority and not for the minority, for whom justice is just a forbidden fruit. That shows that Bentham's distributive justice is nothing but a discriminative justice like that of Hume.

RAWLS' THEORY OF JUSTICE

The liberal theory of justice took a new turn when John Rawls in 1971 published his pioneering work *A Theory of Justice.* In this work, Rawls primarily does two things. First, he provides a corrective to Bentham's utilitarian theory of justice.

Notes

Second, he develops a complete theory (though Amartya Sen calls it 'incomplete') of distributive justice that also includes discriminative justice of a different kind altogether unforeseen by his predecessors. He himself calls his theory a procedural theory of justice, that is, a theory that focuses the ways and means for ensuring social justice. But it may be regarded as a theory of substantive justice as well as it gives sufficient hints about the content of justice.

Rawls considers justice as the most important virtue of institutions, thereby following Plato's assertion that justice is an essential virtue of the State. However, he rejects Plato's thesis that this virtue consists in harmony to be achieved by fixing a static hierarchy among different occupational classes. According to him, this virtue is fairness which may be achieved only when 'primary goods', that is, in his own words 'all social values—liberty and opportunity, income and wealth and the bases of self-respect'—are fairly distributed in a society. Thus, Rawls rejects Benthamite justice, which aims at ensuring maximum happiness for maximum number of people and replaces it by fair distribution of primary goods among all. According to Rawls, the fair distribution of primary goods, which is the key point of his theory of justice, is possible to achieve on the basis of the following principles.

The first principle is that of equal freedom. This means that all will equally enjoy the widest freedom subject to the condition that one's freedom does not, in any way, hinder the enjoyment of freedom by others. Second, all will have equal opportunity in getting the primary goods. If these two principles are followed, then according to Rawls just and equal distribution of primary goods would be possible. Thus, Rawls' justice, far from Bentham's so-called distributive justice for the majority, becomes a truly distributive justice for all. However, he further argues that sometimes, for the sake of fairness, it may be necessary to accept exception to the principle of equal distribution by making room for discrimination. It is in this context that he introduces another principle known as the difference principle. According to this principle, violation of the rule of equal distribution is desirable in a situation where it can be decisively proved that by way of this violation, the least advantaged class is most benefited and placed at par with others; that is, the backward sections of people are entitled to a larger share of primary goods so that, despite the barriers of social stratum, they may get equal treatment with others. Here, Rawls no doubt like Bentham advocates discriminatory justice. But while Bentham is in favour of discrimination against the minority, Rawls' discriminative justice is intended to ensure equal justice for all. It may be interesting to note that 20 years before Rawls came out with this theory, the framers of the Indian Constitution made this discrimination a fundamental rule in favour of the marginal sections of people in Article 15 of the Indian Constitution.

Thus, Rawls' theory of justice has the following features. First, justice is always distributive. Second, if distribution is not equitable, there can be no justice. Third, the final goal of justice is to do good to all equally. Last, in order to lift the socially disadvantaged to the level of the well-off, it is necessary to make special arrangement in favour of the former. This no doubt is to encourage some kind of inequality. But this inequality instead of being adverse to justice is conducive to it.

Three years after Rawls had come out with his theory, it was subjected to substantive criticism by Nozick in a book and Amartya Sen in an essay, each, of course, from his own angle. Nozick rejected Rawls' theory of distributive justice and on this foundation developed his entitlement theory. He dismissed Rawls' principal argument that justice is not possible unless there is a basic change in the distribution system. In fact, he delinked justice from distribution. According to him, an individual as a man has a natural entitlement to enjoyment of certain rights, and justice is meant to safeguard this entitlement. This way, he tried to provide an alternative model to that of Rawls. His model prioritized rights of the individual including the right to property, while Rawls' model laid emphasis on equal social good for all. Nozick was aware that his theory encouraged social inequality, but to him free exercise of the entitled rights was more important than equality, the urge for which, according to him, was born out of envy. Thus, Nozick like Plato envisaged the possibility of justice in an unequal society, which on the modern democratic criterion is no justice at all.

Amartya Sen, in his criticism of Rawls, follows completely a different line of argument. According to him, Rawls' theory is incomplete, as it only provides a critique of Bentham and hence cannot be regarded as an attempt to build up a comprehensive theory of justice. His second criticism is that Rawls' model is incapable of serving as a basis of ethical judgement. Third, he argues, Rawls' theory compares the level of welfare of one with another's but does not take into account the consideration of personal gains and losses. Against the background of these criticisms, he finds little difference between the theories of Bentham and Rawls.

However, with due respect to Sen's genius, it may be replied that Rawls himself claims that his is only a theory of procedural justice, and if Rawls is viewed this way, then it may be said that a theorist whose objective is to lay down the procedure does not have a responsibility to build up a 'complete' theory by filling it with adequate substance and neither is he liable to provide a standard of moral judgement. Again, while finding out ways for improving the level of welfare of one in order to lift him to that of others, some sacrifice on the part of some is surely required and hence, here, the question of personal gains and losses is completely irrelevant. Further, to equate Rawls with Bentham is rather unkind, for each of them viewed justice from his own angle and of course with a different yardstick.

Notes

A NOTE ON THE NATURE OF JUSTICE

It appears from the above survey that although different thinkers at different times have viewed justice differently, they share a common point in that they have all developed institutional justice. That is, they all agree that it requires an institution to establish justice in society. This applies to both Plato, the initiator of the theory of justice, and Rawls, the modern theorist of justice. To Plato, justice essentially is harmony between the different occupational classes of a hierarchical society.

But neither hierarchy nor harmony grows on its own. It is only the State which by its diktat establishes it. Thus, Plato's justice is institutional. So is that of Bentham, another prominent theorist of justice. He makes it plain that his rule of greatest good of the greatest number can be implemented only by the laws of the State. Rawls speaks of equal freedom and equitable distribution of 'primary goods', subject to discrimination in favour of the marginal sections of society, as necessary conditions for ensuring justice. However, all this can be given effect to by State activity.

But howsoever impeccable be the institutional arrangement in this matter, can it be a true guarantee of social justice? The question is much relevant just because of the experiences in real life that institutions can hardly change a man's attitude. Suppose a State is just in its governance and also in its dealings with its citizens. But that does not necessarily make the society just. Again, apparently a society is just when the rules and customs it follows are fair. But that is not all. What is required more is fairness in social relations and social interactions. This is possible only when an individual living in society bears in mind that like him others equally need justice. Therefore, he should consider it his duty to see to it that others also get justice like him. This is where Cicero indeed becomes relevant. According to him, it is not enough that one is treated justly. He should make sure that others also are treated justly.

From this, it obviously follows that justice is no doubt distributive, a view shared by both Aristotle and Rawls. But this distributive justice, to be really meaningful, does require efforts not only at the level of institution but also at the level of the individual. An individual may of course demand justice, but he also has to deserve it. He deserves it only when he admits that others also deserve justice like him and when further he is ready to treat others justly. Thus, justice is possible when all individuals, living in society, have the right attitude for it. An individual must be concerned not only for justice for himself but also for justice for others and must make his own contribution to that effect by his just treatment of others. Hence, it may be said that social justice is of course not only institutional, but it is also attitudinal. It is rather unfortunate that none of the theorists who have deliberated on justice has given attention to this aspect of the matter. Actually, while considering justice in the institutional frame, they have overlooked the role of the individual. On that score, their theories suffer from a limitation.

CONCLUDING OBSERVATIONS

Against the backdrop of what is discussed above, it may now be possible to determine what justice really is. First, political and legal justice are, no doubt, important, but more important than that is social justice. Second, for securing this social justice, it is essential to ensure equal treatment of all. Third, to give effect to this equal treatment, justice is to be distributive. What was initiated by Aristotle and what stands fully modified in the theory of Rawls is indeed true of justice. In other words, justice necessarily signifies equitable distribution of what Rawls has called 'primary goods'. Fourth, justice is not for the majority but for all, and to be fair in this matter, special measures are to be taken for the socially marginal classes of people. Fifth, justice is also institutional. As institutional efforts are the source of legal and political justice, without them social justice cannot be made available. Last, institutional justice alone is no guarantee for social justice for which what is imperative is an appropriate change of attitude on the part of those who are at the receiving end of justice. It is indeed the combination of all these aspects that makes justice truly meaningful.

10

CHAPTER

Law

Notes

INTRODUCTION

Law, like justice, is of very early origin. The idea of law is to be traced back to the late period of ancient Greece when as a result of Roman conquest, Greece lost its independence and became a Roman province. It was in this historical background that Stoic philosophers emerged in Greece. By means of a keen observation of the world of nature, they discovered that the natural world goes by certain rules, universally applicable to all. This discovery led them to the conclusion that, as in the natural world, in the human world also it is possible to introduce a set of universal rules to be applied to all. This is how they were the first to conceive of the idea of law. But as Greece was then a dependent territory, there was naturally no scope to give a concrete shape to this idea. Interestingly, it was the Romans who, assimilating the essence of this Stoic idea, introduced for the first time a system of universal law. No wonder history has recognized Rome as the source of modern jurisprudence.

In modern times, it is found everywhere that people are under compulsion to obey a set of rules made by the State. This is known as law. Thus, State is no doubt the source of law, as its legislative branch makes this law and its judiciary gives recognition to this law, gives effect to it and also guards against its violation. But though State is the chief source of law, it is not the only source, for it is found in every modern State that judiciary gives recognition to customs universally observed by all for long, religious precepts, people's accepted ideas about equity and so on as the source of law as well. Thus, the State creates law but is

Notes

not necessarily the exclusive parent of law. It cannot be denied, however, that without recognition by the judicial organ of the State, law does not get compulsive acceptability. Further, the court is the only agency to give effect to law. Hence, Ernest Barker is right when he defines law as a general body of rules, recognized and enforced by the courts. Thus, law is positive in that it cannot be delinked from the State.

Law is the indubitable means to establish a State's sovereignty over its people. Accordingly, it is by obeying the laws of the State that people render obedience to the sovereign State. In other words, the State by its laws establishes its authority over the individual. Further, the State maintains order in society by means of its laws. This way too the State uses its laws to impose its authority, for State alone is the arbiter to determine how maintenance of order is possible. Viewed from this angle, it appears that the chief purpose of law is to establish authority of the State in society or, to put it differently, laws are the reflection of the supreme power of the State. This actually supports the assertion of Hobbes that law is nothing but command of the sovereign. But this kind of judgement is unfair, as it disregards the true purpose of law. Law is the sum of rules applicable equally to all. But the State cannot arbitrarily make these rules. For instance, if the State makes any law which is clearly against the public interest, then it may apply its coercive power to force the people to obey it for the time being. But it will surely evoke an adverse reaction of the people which in the long run is bound to weaken the authority of the State.

Actually, there is a moral purpose behind every law. Law after all is meant for the people and not for the State. Hence, there is a moral purpose behind law to do good to the people. Bentham was the first philosopher to lay emphasis on this moral purpose of law, though when he applied his 'felicific calculus' (i.e., his principle of greatest good of the greatest number) in determining this moral purpose, he, as explained in the earlier chapter, went wrong. On the other hand, the moral purpose of law was discarded by John Austin, a theorist of the 19th-century England. Austin developed an absolutely positivist view of law in the sense that his opinion was that law is to be viewed only as it is formally seen from outside. Naturally, he denudes law of any moral consideration and takes it just as an order institutionally made by the sovereign State which also by its sovereign power compels people to obey its laws. He further argues that as the State creates laws, it is obviously above law. Law however includes both ordinary law and constitutional law. In view of this political reality, it may be said that the Austinian theory may apply to an autocratic system but not to a democratic system that works on the basis of the assumption that constitution is much above the State and hence is supreme.

Austin's theory of law suffers from such limitation because it follows from his premise that State 'is' the creator of laws. Had it been possible, it may be argued, to delink laws from the State, then perhaps much of the problem could have

Notes

been solved. Perhaps led by this consideration, Henry Maine developed his historical theory of law. In this theory, Maine dismisses the Austinian idea that the State is the creator of law and argues that law is the outcome of a long historical process. According to him, in course of the historical evolution of society, the customs, usages, rites and social rules of a human community have gradually developed and whenever they have assumed an organized shape, they have turned into laws. That is, the legislative and judicial organ of the State, in consideration of their importance and relevance, pick up some of them and give them recognition and this is how law, in an institutional form, comes into being. Thus, the final conclusion of Maine is that the State does not create law; it only recognizes long-standing social mores. Unfortunately, Maine, in his overenthusiasm to delink law from the State, ignores the agreed framework of law. After all, there is no factual evidence to prove that laws only result from social mores. It is a standing reality everywhere that the legislature is the body assigned with the task of making laws, and it does so in consideration of the present needs of society. So it is a gross mistake to claim that legislature while making laws recognizes only the chosen historically developed customs, rites and so on. It does so only in exceptional cases but not usually. Indeed, from whatever angle law is viewed, it is undeniably positive by nature. To that extent, Austin is right, though his failure to view law in its normative aspect is unwarranted.

Harold Laski discards the approach of both Austin and Maine, and develops his own theory of law. He agrees that law is positive. However, he raises the question about the validity of law. In his opinion, law is of course made by the State, but that itself is no ground for its validity. To elaborate, according to him just because a law is made by the State, following the correct institutional procedure, it cannot claim validity. This validity is to be on moral consideration, and the individual alone who is placed under law has the right to determine its validity. In other words, since the individual alone is benefited or harmed by law, he is entitled to assess validity of law on the basis of his moral judgement. In other words, whenever the individual is led by his conscience and power of impartial judgement, he, in the ultimate analysis, is the source of law.

This viewpoint initiated by Laski is more elaborated by Ernest Barker. While analysing law, he has two points to make. First, law by any measure is positive, for it is the legislative organ of the State that makes law and its judicial organ is active in giving effect to it. This is how the imposing authority of the State is validly established in society. This undoubtedly proves the State as the source of law. But this, Barker continues, is not the only source. According to him, law has two sources, one personal and the other impersonal. By personal source is meant the group of persons, who working at the level of the legislature and the judiciary of the State, respectively, create laws and enforce them. The impersonal source on the other hand signifies the moral understanding of the individual affected by law about what is just and what is unjust, and what is fair and what is unfair.

Notes

The personal source gives legal validity to law, while the impersonal source gives it moral validity. To put it differently, as law is made by the State and hence is positive, the individual is under an obligation to render obedience to it. But the individual feels a moral urge to obey it when his capacity of moral judgement informs him that this law is just. These two aspects combined together make law both legally and morally valid. This is epitomized by Barker's oft-quoted statement, 'Authority gives validity to law, and justice gives it value'.

THE STATE AND ITS LAW

A State is known by its laws. That is, to determine the nature and character of a State, one of the most important criteria is its legal system. A State is good if its laws are good, that is, if they are aimed at securing the welfare of the people; it is on the other hand bad if instead of ensuring popular welfare, it serves only the interest of those who make laws. Thus, the system of laws serves as a standard for differentiating a democratic State from a totalitarian State. The laws of a democratic State reflect popular will, while a totalitarian State's laws are made in keeping with the sovereign will of the State. However, sometimes in a democracy, it may so happen that the power that makes law only to serve its political interest, disregarding public interest. In such a case, people of course have a right to freely criticize this law and even to resist it. They also have an ultimate weapon at hand to replace those who run the government by exercising their vote in the next elections. Usually, in apprehension of this electoral weapon of the people, the political authority tries to put itself back on the right track. Needless to add, as this right is not available to the governed in a totalitarian State, the political authority here runs amok with its laws.

Law is undoubtedly related to morality, for as explained above it is the moral purpose of law that gives it validity. In that respect, law is certainly born out of moral consideration. Yet law is not morality. It needs to be distinguished from morality. After all, morality is an outcome of inner self of man. But law is a matter of the external world. On this question, T. H. Green comes very relevant. Although he provides a moral foundation to the authority of the State, including its laws, he desists from confusing law with morality. According to him, law is different from morality in that it is always enforceable, while morality is absolutely incapable of enforcement. Thus, Green first accepts that law is positive and then proceeds to give it a moral dimension.

What may be added, however, is that as the lawmaker of the State is under an obligation to frame laws against the backdrop of a moral consideration, those at the receiving end of laws also have a moral responsibility. After all, it is they who alone are entitled to give true validity to law on the basis of their moral

Notes

judgement as to what is a good law and what is a bad law. But if they are devoid of moral sense to make this judgement or if they refuse to make this moral judgement, the lawmakers are likely to make laws arbitrarily that may go against the general interest. It may be noted, in this connection, that a totalitarian State usually tries to blunt its people's moral sense by using various devices such as false propaganda and brainwash, and also coercive measures. A democratic State, on the other hand, strives to develop among the people a healthy democratic political culture and accordingly the latter always remain alert and vigilant in judging the moral value of law. Thus, it may be concluded that, viewed from either the level of the State or that of the individual, law invariably has a moral support behind it.

NATURE OF LAW

Although in modern society law is recognized as positive, it has behind it a historical legacy of natural law. In ancient times, the idea of natural law was first enunciated by Cicero, a Roman philosopher. He derived the idea of law from the Stoic philosophy. Accordingly, he defined law as based on reason and in consonance with nature. The second part of this definition of course reflects the Stoic influence on him. But if it is omitted, then his definition amounts to suggesting that law is by nature rational and that definitely foreshadows the modern liberal insistence on the moral aspect of law. In the 17th century, however, a different idea of natural law was introduced by the social contract theorists. According to them, natural law is what prevailed in the state of nature that existed prior to the birth of society and State. But as the state of nature they portrayed is just a fiction having no historical evidence in favour of its existence, the idea of natural law they conceived has no practical significance and hence the modern theorists have naturally written it off. But in a different sense, the idea of natural law is still valid, provided it is based on reason, that is, on a moral foundation.

In our times, law is divided into two categories. One is municipal law or national law and the other is international law. Municipal law denotes those laws which a State makes for its people and the jurisdiction of which applies within the territorial boundaries of a State. International law on the other hand is basically applicable in relations between the States of the world. Its chief source is the UN, a world body, and it is composed of the laws of war and peace which, it is expected, will be complied with by all nations. However, there is a basic difference between municipal law and international law. Municipal law is enforceable, but there is till now no mechanism to enforce international law.

Municipal or national law may be of two kinds: one is constitutional law and the other is ordinary law. A constitution embodying fundamental constitutional laws may be the result of a treaty or agreement. Or it may be framed by a duly

Notes

constituted constitution-making body. Further, the legislature of a State is competent to amend the constitution, following the earmarked process and thus makes constitutional laws. Again, constitutional laws may be the result of customs and conventions in case of an unwritten constitution, as in Britain. Moreover, in countries such as the USA and India, where the judiciary is authorized to interpret the constitution, the latter by way of its interpretation may add new meaning to the established constitution and thus judge-made laws may also be a part of the constitutional laws.

Ordinary laws on the other hand are made by the legislature, following duly the law-making procedure as stipulated in the constitution, and it is the task of the judiciary to enforce such laws and take measures in case of their violation. Ordinary laws may be of two kinds: one is private law and the other is public law. Those organizations which have no relation with the functions of the State and are known as private organizations frame rules for their internal administration and for guiding and regulating the functions of their employees. This set of rules is called private law, which is enforced by the management of the private organization. Public law on the other hand is what is made by the law-making organ of the State for rendering services to the people and also for regulating their conduct in case they defy the rules of the game. This is known as statutory law that is directly related to individual and society. However, when a public law determines the composition and functions of public administration, and also regulates the relation between the administrative authority and the citizens, it is called administrative law.

It is evident from the above analysis that law is an important aspect of the State. As shown earlier, the State is an intangible idea, mostly used for theoretical convenience. However, law is one of the available means to establish the identity of the State in actual practice, or in other words law is the mirror of the State. Further, that the State holds and exercises power substantially is reflected through the making and working of law. Thus, it may with reason be concluded that where there is no law, there is no State.

11 CHAPTER

Citizenship

Notes

INTRODUCTION

Persons living in the territory of a State are not necessarily citizens. Only those of them who are recognized as members of the State are citizens. This recognition is, of course, given by the State on several grounds. The chief among them is descent and residence. That is, if one is born of a citizen or if he is born in the territory of a State, he will be recognized as a citizen. When recognized this way, he is regarded as a natural citizen. But one can be a naturalized citizen as well. When the State grants citizenship to a non-citizen, provided he has fulfilled certain conditions specified by the State, the latter is regarded as a naturalized citizen. There is no fixed standard for determining these conditions. The rule regarding this varies from country to country. However, the practice of granting naturalized citizenship is in vogue in all modern democratic countries. Usually, no distinction is made between a natural citizen and a naturalized citizen. The latter is entitled to all the rights enjoyed by the former.

A citizen is known by the rights he is allowed to exercise. The most important of these rights is the right to freely exercise his political choice, that is, the right to vote and the right to seek and hold political power, irrespective of his social status. This at least is true of modern democracy. It is interesting to note that even in the slave society of ancient Greece, citizenship was treated as a matter of theoretical concern. Although Plato in his works seems to have no interest in the idea of citizenship, his celebrated disciple Aristotle, in his *Politics,* developed a theory of citizenship. According to Aristotle, a citizen is he who has the capacity to participate actively in the deliberative and judicial functions of the State, and it is this capacity that makes one a good citizen. To him, thus participation in the political process is the basic criterion for determining citizenship and to that extent, his idea of citizenship seems to have some similarity with the modern definition of citizenship. However, he eventually drifts away from the modern view when he considers the too young, the too old and also the women as incapable of citizenship which by and large offends the spirit of modern democracy committed to universal suffrage. Finally, true to the temper of his society, Aristotle argues that to make a good use of their rights, citizens need sufficient leisure and accordingly they would be freed from all work involving manual labour to attend to which is the responsibility alone of the slaves who are permanently denied the right of citizenship. This clearly reveals that in his theory of citizenship, Aristotle was a child of his time, as his citizenship is not a right but only a privilege as it is meant for slave owners and not for others.

In conformity with the system of universal law they developed, for the first time the Romans initiated the legalistic view of citizenship in that, according to them, citizenship involves the right to have equality before law. That was no doubt an improvement over Aristotle's theory. Second, they extended citizenship to the people of their dependent territories, which was of course a significant step forward at that time. Third, like Aristotle they stood for participatory citizenship; that is, according to them citizenship denotes participation in public affairs. However, unlike in Aristotelian theory, this was participation only in military services. But in any case whatever advancement the Romans made with regard to the idea of citizenship, it was ultimately flawed by the limitations of their slave society. To them, as to Aristotle, citizenship was a prohibited enclave for the slaves.

In the mediaeval period, deliberate efforts on the part of the Church to disseminate a firm belief among the people of Christian faith that everything of their life and around was determined by God's will led to a conviction that temporal matters like citizenship are of no relevance and that people should rest content with the fact that they were not citizens but brethren of one Christian world. However, Marsilius of Padua who emerged at a time when the Middle Age was about to come to an end and who thus served as a connecting link between the mediaeval and modern ideas felt the need of citizenship. He argued that it is the consent of citizens that determines to what extent a government is good and stable. Further, he rejected the idea of direct representation of citizens in the political process and favoured their indirect representation which in later times became the basis of modern democracy. In the post-Renaissance period, Machiavelli and Bodin brought into focus the question of citizenship. Machiavelli's emphasis was on the qualities of a citizen. According to him, to be

Notes

a true citizen one needs to be led by patriotism, self-restraint, reverence and also the proclivity to put primacy on public interest instead of on private interest. But to the question on what grounds a person is entitled to be a citizen, he had no answer. Bodin on the other hand seemed to be much closer to the modern idea when he identified birth and enfranchisement as the way of acquiring citizenship. Finally, when under the influence of liberalism democracy took an organized shape, citizenship began to be regarded as a vital aspect of the State, and it was universally accepted that consent of citizens through their indirect representation envisages the fundamental characteristic of a democratic political system.

CHARACTERISTICS OF A CITIZEN

In modern democracy, citizenship is reflective of a man's identity as a political man. As a political man, he deserves rights to assert himself against the authority of the State. These rights are political rights that include political freedom and political equality. Political freedom mainly involves freedom to organize politically, freedom to criticize and even to resist political authority subject to the condition that it will not invite disorder or anarchy, freedom of political participation and freedom of political choice. Political equality on the other hand envisages conditions where all citizens may enjoy and exercise their political freedom equally, that is, notwithstanding whether a citizen is of high or low origin or whether he is much propertied or very poor. It is the availability of these opportunities that not only differentiates democracy from an autocratic system but also helps measure the merit of a democracy. Thus, it may be said that an effective citizenship is the real test of democracy.

Who is a good citizen is a question that has been a matter of concern to political theorists since Aristotle. To this question, Aristotle gives a very simple answer. According to him, a good citizen is he who is capable to rule and of being ruled. But this is an emphasis only on capacity and not on quality. Indeed, it is no answer to the question, for in modern democracy it is always found that every citizen has a right to be a part of governance and he is as well ready to be subjected to such governance. Yet every citizen can hardly be regarded as a good citizen. Thus, Aristotle's answer, it may be said, is not only simple but simplistic as well. St Thomas Aquinas, a 13th-century mediaeval philosopher, did not believe that to be a good citizen one does necessarily have to be a good man. To that extent, he was of course right in that he treated citizenship as purely a political question freed from moral considerations. But he did not elaborate what makes one a good citizen. On the other hand, T. H. Green in the 19th century brought back a moral dimension to citizenship as he implied man only as a moral being, that is, as one who accepts moral responsibility for his act, deserves citizenship. Modern democracy discards all these viewpoints. In modern democracy, it

Notes

appears citizenship is purely a political question as it is delimited by political rights an individual enjoys. However, it underscores the fact that although all its citizens enjoy equal political rights, all are not equally good citizens. In this context, it focuses the qualities needed to make one a good citizen. These qualities are political consciousness, political knowledge, enthusiastic willingness for political participation and, last but not the least, the level of literacy, particularly in countries like India where illiteracy is yet a social problem. Thus, if citizens are not aware of the value of their citizenship and also of the political rights citizenship enjoins, if they lack proper knowledge about the governing process and show any apathy to participate politically, they cannot be good citizens as they will often fault in the exercise of the rights of their citizenship. Literacy however is no problem in advanced Western societies and accordingly most of the citizens there are able to live up to the needs of citizenship. But in India, where more than 30 per cent of people are yet illiterate and therefore politically ignorant, the power seekers are often found to apply many unholy means to deceive and confuse members of electorate. What miracle can literacy do may on the contrary be exemplified by the voting behaviour of the people of Kerala, a southern state of India. People of Kerala, the only Indian state officially recognized as fully literate, by way of their political knowledge and consciousness have been able to generate an electoral atmosphere so good that during elections, they can freely exercise their political choice without any undue interference by the power seekers. Not only that, the citizens of Kerala have so well viewed periodic elections as an instrument of political change that no party there can manage to stay in power for more than one term.

DUTIES AND RIGHTS OF A CITIZEN

As citizens have rights, they have duties as well. Their first duty is to the State. A citizen is under a permanent obligation to render his obedience to the government of the State which grants him citizenship together with the rights accompanying it. This, of course, does not mean total surrender as in a totalitarian system. As a citizen is armed with his political rights, he has a right to criticize the government and also to resist and replace it. However, he also has a duty to himself and others. He has a duty to himself in the sense that he must be conscious of the value of his citizenship and try to be a good citizen. Accordingly, he should orient his personal life in such a way that he may grow into a politically conscious and politically knowledgeable person, and also attain a certain standard of education. In this matter, the State also has a duty to its citizens in that it must devise a mechanism for enforcing and protecting the rights of its citizens, and also ensure an environment where a citizen gets ample opportunities for developing political consciousness and also having political knowledge and education. It may be relevant to mention in this connection that in view of this duty, the Constitution of India by virtue of its 86th Amendment has

Notes

arranged free and compulsory education for all children up to the age of 14 years so that in later life they may grow up as good citizens. Further, a citizen has a duty to others in that he must see that his rights as a citizen do not harm the exercise of similar rights by other citizens. Thus, citizenship is marked by rights and duties.

A good citizenship alone is not enough; what is needed more is effective citizenship. An effective citizen is he who not at other's biddings but out of his own willingness is an active citizen. That is, one who actively participates in the current political process by freely exercising his rational choice is an effective citizen. It is this effective citizenship that maintains to a large extent the merit of democracy. To illustrate, if a citizen exercises his right of political choice rather passively, for instance, if he casts his vote under duress or at the behest of others without applying free rational judgement, democracy though retains its form loses indeed its validity. Thus, effective citizenship is a guarantee of a good democratic government.

So far we have discussed citizenship in terms of political rights a citizen enjoys. But a citizen has social rights as well. The most important of these social rights is the right of a citizen to establish the distinctiveness of his identity as a citizen in the society and to integrate this identity with that of other citizens living in the society. It is this integration that leads to the emergence of all citizens as a distinctive group in the society that provides to the youngsters a lesson as to what they should do and how they should behave whenever in due time they become citizens. There are some who are of the opinion that citizenship should represent various groups with different social and cultural identities. But social and cultural identities are relevant in the context of a social man and not a political man. Hence, if citizenship is taken as basically revealing the identity of a political man, this theory obviously falls through. Again, however conventional it may sound, the fact is that a person living in a State is recognized as a citizen individually and not as a member of a group. Thus, acquisition and loss of the rights of citizenship applies to an individual and not as a member of a group. Similarly, rules of making a naturalized citizen are meant for an individual and not for a group. So the view of citizenship as a group may be regarded as false. Accordingly, when I. M. Young in his essay 'Polity and Group Difference' published in 1989 introduced the concept of 'differentiated citizenship', it was difficult to accept its validity. His argument in favour of this idea is that the marginalized section of the people of society are brought under the purview of citizenship only as a group. True, the marginalized people are subjected to many difficulties arising out of unkind social precepts. But, thanks to the universal suffrage of modern society, each of them gets political rights as an individual and not as a group as such. Hence, citizenship is universally applicable to all, irrespective of social inequality and social injustice suffered by the marginalized groups.

Notes

CITIZENSHIP: NEW DIMENSIONS

In the present century, certain striking worldwide developments have brought a new meaning and dimension to citizenship. These developments may be identified as globalization, introduction of market economy in almost all the countries of the world including even China, which still clings to the signpost of socialism, and the growing anxiety about deterioration of global environment. These three developments, originating in the last quarter of the last century, are now recognized as basic world realities which no nation or, for that matter, no national can ignore.

Globalization economically has broken all national barriers ensuring free flow of capital across the world. This together with the free play of market economy has made the world much narrower in the present century. Thus, it is now a common sight that an individual who is a citizen of a particular State freely invests and does business in another State.

Similarly, goods made in a foreign country freely compete with indigenously manufactured commodities and thus consumers of a country have been habituated to a wide use of foreign goods, which in the past under the influence of a strong national spirit was treated as rather an anathema by them. Again, the problems of global warming and environment pollution have been casting a gloom on the future of people belonging to every nation. As a result, people all over the world are increasingly realizing what a great danger it portends for them. Naturally, it is now a matter of common concern to all humans inhabiting the earth.

It may be noted that the UN, which as a world body came into being more than 70 years ago with its avowed object of freeing the world from the scourge of war and establishing international peace and international spirit, has miserably failed in fulfilling its purpose. During all these years, there has been an unholy nuclear arms race and frequent armed clashes and conflicts among different countries, with the UN remaining as a passive spectator. This is a clear evidence of the failure of the UN to bring people out of the slough of narrow nationalism and establish firmly the idea of world citizenship. It may be said that though the UN has failed politically the present world scenario economically has brought success. Indeed, the recent developments noted above have brought in realities that are encouraging citizens of a country to view themselves as a part of the world. That is, a citizen is no longer only the citizen of a State but is also a world citizen. So it may be said that time has now come to evolve a theory of world citizenship that will help a citizen view himself against a larger perspective.

Notes

It may be added that natural citizens who constitute the majority of the citizen body become citizens not by their deliberate choice. They are rather destined to be citizens of a State. Only the naturalized citizens exercise their choice to be the citizens of a State. Viewed that way, it should be admitted that Aristotle was right when he said that man, unless he is a beast or a god, must be a member of the State. But this shows that the source of citizenship is no doubt the State. However, the State has a basic duty to provide external conditions so that by taking advantage of these conditions, a citizen may grow into a good citizen. Thus, the citizen and the State stand on a common plane sharing duties with each other.

As noted earlier, T. H. Green's attempt to give a moral dimension to citizenship is untenable because citizenship in any case is the result of positive laws made by the State. Yet it cannot be denied that a citizen has a moral responsibility to be a good and effective citizen. True, as seen above, good and effective citizenship does not denote any moral virtue. But as a citizen has a moral responsibility in this regard, there is surely a moral perspective of citizenship and on that score Green's theory cannot altogether be dismissed.

12

CHAPTER

Political Culture

INTRODUCTION

Notes

The idea of political culture is of recent origin. It evolved in the post-Second World War period in the 20th century. However, in a sense its roots may be traced to the ideas of Aristotle. While prescribing the preventives of revolution, Aristotle suggested that one of the ways to forestall revolution in the State is to educate people in concordance with the spirit of the constitution. By this, what he meant to say was that a State attains stability when its people develop a mindset apt to obey the authority of the prevailing State. Two things are implicit in this prescription. First, the State has a direct hand in orienting its people to accept legitimacy of its authority. Second, not only objective conditions but also subjective conditions are necessary for the sustenance of a political system. The concept of political culture, it may be said, rejects the first but absorbs the second.

Those who introduced the idea of political culture meant it to be a contrivance, useful for comparing one political system with the other. According to them, every political system has its own political culture, and the specificity of this culture is the hallmark of its character. Every political system, they further argue, has an objective framework and a subjective framework. The objective framework comprises the constitutional and ordinary laws, the structure and functions of government and so on, and favourable attitudes and orientations of a people towards the political system represent the subjective framework. It is the combination of these two frameworks that bears the identity of a political system.

Political culture is thus defined as a conglomerate of perception, attitude and orientation of a people with regard to a political system. Put in simpler terms, it means nothing but an emotional and attitudinal attachment of people to the political authority, adding strength to the latter. In other words, political culture is a means to legitimize the authority of a State. Those who ideate on political culture are emphatic in their point that political culture is not the outcome of any deliberate attempt on the part of the State to grow it and hence it is spontaneous. It is true that political culture is not indoctrination. Yet the fact is that the State of course has a hand behind its development. After all, those who run a political system are always found to be keen on developing an educational system, and also promoting and fostering by various means a kind of social and cultural milieu, contributory to the smooth running of the system. Unlike in a totalitarian State, in a democracy, this of course is not done in a very visible way but rather subtly. And that proves that political culture is not wholly spontaneous.

It is futile to expect that despite the best efforts on the part of political authority, political culture will develop among the illiterate and ignorant people living in a traditional society and led by traditional beliefs, for these traditional beliefs build a permanent high wall between these people and the political system with the result that there is virtually no communication between the two. This naturally gives no scope to these people to have any knowledge about the political system, though this knowledge is the primary condition for the development of political culture. Thus, political culture better develops in a society that is free from traditional outlook, that is, more or less modernized.

Once people attain knowledge about the political system, the process does not stop but continues further, for on the basis of this knowledge people begin to develop their feelings about the system. It may be a feeling of acceptance or rejection. If this acceptance or rejection is under the influence of external forces, that is, not on the basis of reasoned calculation on the part of the people but under duress or by means of political propaganda or any political trick, then certainly it is not spontaneous but made by deliberate attempt on the part of those who run the political system and hence it cannot be treated as an element of political culture but rather as an aspect of political indoctrination. Further, after this feeling of acceptance or rejection is developed, there is another step to generate political culture. That step is evaluation of the political system. That is, people must be capable of making a value judgement. This means that people by means of their rational judgement should be able to develop a sense of values, on the criterion of which they can make sure why they develop a favourable or adverse orientation towards the political system. Further, by virtue of this evaluative criterion, they may know well in what respect their political culture is different

Notes

from the political culture in other political systems. This implies two things. First, the individuals living under a political system must be sufficiently conscious individuals. Second, political culture thus developed is an important means to distinguish one political system from the other.

Political culture may be of two types—holistic and fragmentative. When political culture comprises political orientations to the political system as a whole, reigning over the society, it may be called holistic. On the other hand, in a democracy at least various political organizations such as political parties and pressure groups grow and function around the political system, and they together with the political system represent the political process. People's attitude and orientations to each of these political organizations may be regarded as fragmentative. As hinted earlier, political culture may not necessarily be compliant to the political system and the political organizations. Sometimes people in their attitude and orientations may consciously be in an aversive mood in regard to them. Hence, political culture may further be classified into positive and negative. A compliant political culture may be called positive, while an adverse political culture may be viewed as negative political culture. Again, although theoretically political culture may be treated as homogeneous in actual practice, it is far from so. After all, variety of attitude and opinion among a people can hardly be denied. Thus, it may so happen that one section of people represents positive culture, while the other develops a negative political culture. Further, a positive political culture may relate to the political system or to the political organizations developing in society. The same may be true of negative political culture. On this consideration, political culture may be classified into four categories, namely positive-holistic political culture, positive-fragmentative political culture, negative-holistic political culture and negative-fragmentative political culture.

ORIGIN OF A POLITICAL CULTURE

Although political culture is wholly related to politics, its birthplace, however, is not the State but society. Naturally, the culture prevailing in a society or, it may be said, social culture serves as the background for the development of political culture. If the dominant culture of a society leads its people to be involved more in social affairs with least concern for political objects, then the odds are that they will have little willingness to develop any perception about political matters or they will have a false perception about political objects. This kind of situation still prevails in India's rural society. People living in rural India with agriculture as their principal occupation are found to be living in a small and insular world where they tend to treat their agricultural activities as the centre of their social interaction, and political objects hardly enter into their stagnant life processes.

Notes

Obviously, the political system or for that matter the functions of various political organizations centring round the political system are of little interest to them. Even when they come in contact with the dynamics of political process, they invariably develop a misperception. Thus, it is found that to an individual living in rural India, government means only a local tax collector or a local agricultural or irrigation official or at best the block development officer of the area. This seems to suggest that political culture, at least, in India is mostly an urban phenomenon.

However, in removing this limitation of rural society as regards the healthy growth of political culture, India's media, in recent times, have been playing quite an important role. Of course, unlike the largely urbanized Western societies, India's rural society inhabited mostly by illiterate people obviously benefits very little from the print media in having political knowledge and consciousness. But the massive spread of the electronic media, particularly the TV, introduced in India in the early 1970s and fast diversified in the subsequent decades has wrought virtually a mental revolution among the rural people of India in as far as the television's visuals have brought them in direct contact with political personalities and political happenings. As a result, India's rural people are now in a better position in that, thanks to the TV news channels, they seem to have at least a reasonable amount of political knowledge.

However, it is difficult to agree that on the basis of this knowledge, they are capable of developing their attitude of acceptance or rejection and finally can make an evaluative judgement. Because that requires a reason-oriented capacity, which knowledge itself cannot generate.

Talking about the media, it must be admitted that all over the world today, media are playing a very important role in helping people have political knowledge as well as their orientation to and evaluation of political objects. This shows that in respect of political culture, media have not only an instrumental role but also a generative role. That is, media of course assist the process of development of political culture. But at the same time, they act as a source of political culture. People generally believe what is printed in newspapers or telecasted by the 'idiot box'. Taking advantage of this general credibility, media usually try to shape and influence the political orientation of readers and viewers, and to a large measure they are successful on that score. This is how media serve as a source of political culture. But this augurs a danger too. True, as the 'fourth estate' media have a recognized responsibility of guiding people along the right track and thereby creating public attitude and opinion on the ongoing political process. But it is frequently noticed that they do this job not without bias. Hence, there is a great chance that they encourage a misdirected political culture based on deceit or falsehood.

Notes

This is what brings us to the role of the individual vis-à-vis political culture. As noted earlier, political culture is rooted in a society. This is why even in the case of democratic political systems, political culture differs from one to another depending on the nature of the society concerned, as is found in UK and India, the two parliamentary democratic systems. But society, in the final analysis, is an association of individuals. Hence, it may be said that individual is the ultimate source of political culture. That is, though political culture operates at the macro level, it actually originates at the micro level. But political culture may originate at the micro level only when the individual develops certain qualities. First, he must be educated enough to understand the ins and outs of politics of the country. Second, he must not have apathy to national politics. That is, he must not be a passive observer of political activities going around but should be a watchful observer of politics and active participant in the activities required of him as a citizen. Third, he must develop a power of rational judgement whereby he may discern the right and wrong of the political system and the political process. Last, he must be free from all biases while making this evaluation.

EVOLUTION OF POLITICAL CULTURE

Political culture results out of consensus. That is, political culture is by nature consensual. Unless the attitudes and orientations of a people reach a point of convergence, there cannot be political culture in the truest sense of the term. This convergence is possible when the society that serves as the broad canvas of political culture is more or less homogeneous. For instance, in Britain the society is not marked by too many diversities and divergences. Further, the insularity of Britain has led its people to be firmly tied in a common bond. Accordingly, it is easy to achieve consensus in British society, and hence a strong and unchanging political culture has developed in Britain. Quite contrary is the scene in India. Since India is a multi-racial, multi-religious, multi-lingual and multi-cultural country, one notices not just one homogeneous society but many societies with their respective distinctiveness in its different geographical areas. Thus, social conditions, complementary to consensus, are conspicuous by their absence in India. True, the parliamentary democratic system at work, both at the Centre and in the states of India, ensures common political conditions. However, despite these common political conditions, it appears that in different political regions of India, sometimes regional feelings grow much stronger so much so that there is a demand for political autonomy at par with the separate historical and cultural identity of the area. Thus, in a country like India within the framework of a general political culture there often grow sectional political cultures, making it impossible to treat the overall political culture as homogeneous, since it by any measure is heterogeneous. Hence, political culture may further be classified into homogeneous and heterogeneous.

Notes

Usually, political culture is in congruence with the political system and the political entities associated with this system. In fact, that is how political culture adds strength to the political system and all political structures. But in abnormal situations, it may so happen that a part of political culture delinks itself from the mainstream and challenges the entire system together with its adjuncts. Thus, political culture may also be classified into compliant political culture and incongruent political culture. The incongruent political culture, however, does not grow spontaneously. It generally originates and gathers strength under the behest of an extraordinary personality or a party committed to a particular ideology. For instance, in British India the rulers took to various measures—some of them salutary, no doubt—to develop across the country a compliant political culture. But with the emergence of Gandhi and the application of his unique political strategies, an incongruent political culture gradually became very strong that busted the foundation of British rule in India.

Compliant political culture however is related to an independent political system, for unless people are recognized free citizens of a State, it is preposterous to expect that they would spontaneously develop an agreeable attitude and orientation towards the political objects at work around them. This however implies a responsibility on the part of those who run or help running the political system. They should have a mechanism whereby knowledge about the entire political process freely flows to all levels of society. Second, they should extend educational facilities to all sections of people so that it is easier for the latter to attain political knowledge.

Third, they should encourage the development of an uninhibited social environment where people may freely interact with each other and exchange with others of the society their knowledge, ideas and orientations. If the power sincerely attends to such responsibility, those at the receiving end are likely to develop a compliant mood and attitude with regard to the former.

Apparently, political culture may look similar to nationalism. But actually political culture is much different from nationalism, for nationalism is unidimensional while political culture is multi-dimensional. Nationalism grows out of a people's emotional attachment to their nation. Since nationalism involves only emotion, there is little of rationality in it and there is hardly any scope of evaluative judgement in it. Hence, it is easy to evoke the spirit of nationalism. Political culture, on the other hand, is a much complex process. As noted earlier, it is composed of several elements. However, mere presence of these elements is not enough to give birth to political culture. It takes a definitive shape only when these elements are actively and consciously utilized with a view to adding strength to the ongoing political process. Further, nationalism is static while political culture is a dynamic process. The spirit of nationalism does not change; it stays at a certain point. On the contrary, political culture is a changing process.

Notes

Since history is one of its important determinants, it changes with the change of history, political, social, economic and cultural. To illustrate, the case of India may be cited. When India became an independent and sovereign State because of the strongest emotional attachment of the people to it, political culture was purely positive and compliant. But as Indian democracy gradually began developing, leaving its impact on the various facades of social life, its political culture no longer remained absolutely compliant as incongruent political culture began showing its face. Today, in the 21st century against the backdrop of globalization and India's free market economy, India's political culture has taken a new route. It is now both compliant and incongruent.

POLITICAL CULTURE AND POLITICAL SYSTEM

Although a changing process, political culture is a permanent feature of a political system, hence the question: How does it continue generation after generation? To account for this continuity, another concept which like political culture is also of recent origin has been introduced by modern theorists. This concept is known as political socialization. Political socialization denotes the process by which political culture is transmitted from one generation to another and thus maintains the continuity of political culture in a system. Thus, political socialization is a vital aspect of political culture. The process of political socialization does not stop at a particular point of time. It represents a continuum. That is, it goes on continuously as a river flows for ever.

To understand better the nature of political socialization, it is essential to distinguish it from political learning. Political learning means learning about politics by someone from someone. That is, it is a bilateral process involving two clearly identifiable actors, one giving the learning and the other receiving it. This shows that political learning is a deliberate and conscious process. One who furnishes the substance of political learning at his choice does it deliberately. On the other hand, he who learns this stuff of course receives it consciously. But political socialization is neither a deliberate nor a conscious process. When a source transmits political culture from one generation to the other, it is not that he decides to do it. Often he is not even aware that he is involved in this task of transmission. Actually, it is through his manifest behaviour that political socialization takes place. Thus, by no means it is his deliberate act. On the other hand, one who is at the receiving point of this transmission does not act consciously to assimilate it. Somehow he is influenced by what he receives and habitually internalizes it.

By its task of transmission, political socialization of course maintains the continuity and stability of political culture. But sometimes it helps in transforming and even creating political culture. For instance, those who run a political

Notes

system may decide to change its track by means of new principles and ideologies. This obviously calls for a new political environment to sustain that what is necessary is a prompt change in people's political attitudes and orientations. The standing political culture is itself unable to accommodate such changes. This is where political socialization may play a significant role. By transfusing newer ideas within the existing political culture, it may quickly recreate political culture suited for the new environment. This may be illustrated by citing the recent happenings in Indian democracy. Indian democracy in recent times has undergone a visible transformation by opening the gates for globalization and by introducing the free market economy. This indeed has ushered in a new kind of political environment. To harmonize people's orientations with this environment, political socialization has no doubt played a vital role to the effect that globalization and market economy have earned fast popular acceptability. To what extent political socialization will be successful in this mission depends much on the powerful leadership at the top of the political system concerned, national and international conditions, and also the flexibility and pliability of people's political attitude and orientations.

Political socialization may basically be of two types: direct or manifest and indirect or latent. When knowledge, values, attitudes and orientations of purely political nature are straightaway transmitted from one generation to other, it is called direct or manifest political socialization. When on the other hand the content of such attitudes, orientations and so on is not overtly political but is implicitly related somehow to what may be applicable in the political domain, it may be regarded as indirect or latent political socialization. For instance, when a person gathers some political knowledge from the media or by attending the meeting of a political party, he may be said to be directly socialized politically. Again, by reading the autobiography of say Gandhi, when someone develops the idea that truth and honesty are the two fundamental virtues of man and subsequently is led to form the opinion that politics should be founded on truth and honesty, the political socialization he undergoes may be regarded as latent or indirect.

There are some who make a distinction between intentional political socialization and unintentional political socialization (which the present author too has done in one of his earlier works on political sociology). But truly speaking, this is a false distinction. As noted earlier, political culture to a large extent is spontaneous in normal conditions of a democracy. Only in abnormal conditions it is deliberately created, that is, is intentional. Similarly, in normal conditions political socialization is not intentional. Actually, it grows through a natural process by means of interpersonal relations and social interactions. It is not that one particular generation consciously and deliberately transmits its political culture to the next generation. This transmission in fact takes place through the intimacy and interactions between the two.

Notes

Those who theorize on political socialization identify certain agencies through which political socialization is effected. These agencies according to them are family, peer groups, educational institutions, secondary groups, government and its organs, party agencies and the media. This virtually amounts to suggesting that political socialization follows from certain sources. But if political socialization is not intentional, then it is of no use to pinpoint its sources. After all, a family does not deliberately inculcate political knowledge and political values among its youngsters. So is the case as regards educational institutions, peer groups, secondary groups, government and the media. None of them directly transmits political culture. Even the media take it as their task to provide political information and their analysis of political facts without ever regarding it as their duty to transmit political culture. Hence, it would be improper to treat them as agencies or sources of political socialization. What in fact they together do is to provide a broad forum facilitating easy and continuous interaction among the people that in effect helps the process of political socialization.

Thus, it may be concluded that political socialization is an indispensable handmaid of political culture. But as political culture is more or less spontaneous, political socialization is free from any outside intervention. It represents a continuous flow that goes on uninhibited, adding stability and continuity to political culture.

13 CHAPTER

Democracy

Notes

INTRODUCTION

When the Second World War ended with the victory of allied powers against the axis powers, it was universally recognized as a triumph of democracy against fascism. This also carried an optimism that thence forward, democracy would continue having a long triumphant march without any hindrance. But the hope was belied. Soon after, the emergence of socialist Soviet Union as a big power equally vying with democratic big power, the USA, and the birth of Soviet satellite States as well as coming into being of socialist China subjected the democratic system to a new challenge from socialism. With the availability of political options, some of the emerging nations of Asia, Africa and Latin America leaned towards socialism, and a hot debate continued on the question: Which one was a better system, democracy or socialism? However, all the debate ended when in the early 1990s socialism collapsed in the Soviet Union and its satellite States, and China followed suit with its overt abandonment of socialist ideology albeit holding out socialism as its signpost. Thus, today in the 21st century democracy is a political system with no parallel, left unchallenged and undisturbed.

Democracy as we find it today has behind it a history of a little more than 300 years. However, hundreds of years ago in ancient Greek society, democracy was found to be at work. This is well vouched by the ancient Greek city state of Athens where under the historic leadership of Pericles in the 4th century BC

Notes

democracy achieved notable success. But Athenian democracy, marked by David Held as classical democracy, had little in common with modern democracy. It was a direct democracy characterized by citizens' direct participation in deliberative functions of government, while modern democracy is invariably an indirect democracy based on the principle of popular representation. Interestingly, although democracy germinated in the early Greek society, it got no theoretical support from the two great philosophical masters of the era—Plato and Aristotle—despite the fact that both of them got ample opportunity to closely watch the contemporary Athenian democracy. Plato reposed all his faith on rule by aristocrats, and Aristotle viewed democracy as a bad form of government taking it as a rule by the poor and opted for rule by the middle class which he called polity.

AS A FORM OF GOVERNMENT

Democracy for long was used to be treated as a form of government. Even today, there is a general tendency to view democracy more as a type of government based on the principle of popular sovereignty and practice of popular representation effected by periodic elections. But it is too narrow a view. Actually, the connotative canvas of democracy is much larger that includes, besides a democratic government, a democratic attitude and environment and a democratic society. That is, democracy is more a way of life than a form of government. This way of life must be reflected in the attitude and activities of those who govern, in the behaviour and sense of values of the governed and in effective development of a democratic society. This suggests that the worth of democracy depends on fulfilment of quite a few conditions.

Historically, democratic government and party system have gone hand in hand. No wonder modern democratic political system works mainly with the aid of a party system. Thus, in a presidential democracy the aspirants for the office of chief executive fight elections as party nominees and he who gets majority of votes in elections occupies office for a certain period. On the other hand, in this system those who seek to be members of the legislature which functions independent of the executive and wields considerable power fight elections also as party nominees. In a parliamentary democracy on the other hand, the nominees of various political parties contest in elections to be members of the legislature, and the party bagging majority of seats in the legislature sends its chosen members to form the executive that governs for a fixed term. However, unlike in a presidential democracy, the executive in the parliamentary system cannot work independent of the legislature. It always remains collectively responsible to the legislature. This means that in case the executive loses confidence of the majority of members in the lower house of the legislature, it has to resign. Thus, the two

Notes

integral parts of a modern representative democracy are party system and periodic elections.

In a modern democracy, members of the executive who are in exclusive charge of governance cannot disavow a couple of obligations. For instance, first they must maintain an attitude oriented by the democratic ideal that imbibes a people's government. Thus, while governing they must be led by the spirit that they are always in service to the people and not to themselves and the parties they represent, and hence cannot ever disregard people's voice and public interest. The second obligation which follows from the first is that they cannot act arbitrarily. They must do what people want them to do and desist from going headstrong. This precisely calls for a perfectly rational behaviour on the part of power holders in a democracy. Indeed, viewed from this angle democracy is a government of reason, by reason and for reason.

In advanced democracies of the West, this maxim is found to be more or less followed. Thus, in a parliamentary democracy like Britain, it is noticed that prime minister as the chief executive hardly strives to establish his personal dominance or charisma (barring some exceptions like that of Winston Churchill and Margaret Thatcher, of course). He along with his ministers runs the government in a straitjacketed manner, strictly complying with rules, norms and standing conventions. In a presidential democracy on the other hand the president as the lone executive, in the absence of his accountability to the legislature, has immense scope to act arbitrarily and lionize his personal image. But save for a few stray examples such as Theodore Roosevelt and Donald Trump, unbroken loyalty to the letter and spirit of the constitution as well as to democratic values and culture acts as a brake on his going beyond the limits.

As already noted, political parties serve as an indispensable adjunct of a democratic system. Indeed, without political parties democracy cannot work. But that does not mean that political parties are an indomitable juggernaut to serve as an overlord of democracy. Political parties of course play a vital role in constituting the legislature and forming the executive. That is, political parties are the main actor in democratic elections. But therein ends its main function. Once these functions are over, their duty is to go backstage. That is, if democracy is to remain true to its ideal and meaning, political parties must voluntarily accept self-abandonment from the domain of legislative and executive decision-making. In between two periodic elections, they of course may draw up strategies and act accordingly, but in any case they cannot interfere with the ongoing governmental process. In Western democracies, this indeed is the standing norm political parties faithfully follow. After elections are over and the government is formed, they virtually go into hibernation until the bell for the next elections begins tolling. On the other hand, the government though essentially a party government is never a stooge to the party. It tries to function not as an

Notes

agent of the party but rather as an agent of the people. Thus in the West, democracy runs on the basis of an agreed job division—the government governs and political parties keep trying by various ways to win over people to its side.

People should not only desire democracy but also deserve it. To be deserving for democracy, they have to take upon themselves a great burden of responsibility. Indeed, the success of democracy to a large extent depends on how they act and behave. In their political behaviour or for that matter in discharging their democratic responsibilities as citizens, they ought to be fearless led by rational judgement and rational choice. After all, it is they who are the primary architect of two of the main organs of a democratic government—legislature and executive. Hence, the quality and efficiency of those who run these two organs depend much on how rationally people exercise their choice in constituting these two organs. In other words, if in their voting behaviour they are led by their own rational judgement and not influenced by campaign and propaganda of political parties, democracy in all likelihood may produce a good government. Thus, it may be debatable whether democracy by nature is good or bad, but what is above debate is the fact that it is the people who make a democratic government good or bad. However, two conditions are necessary in order that people may play this role desired of them. First, they must have adequate political consciousness so that they may be politically knowledgeable and neutral observer of the political happenings around. Second, they must have mental strength enough to withstand all political allurement and pressure. Thus, it may be said that in the final analysis a sound individual is the eternal sentinel of democracy.

DEMOCRACY AND THE THIRD WORLD

Democracy no doubt has been more or less a success in the West, traditionally regarded as its playfield. But the record is not that bright in the emerging nations of the Third World. Most of these nations of course after Independence started their political journey with a democratic government. But this journey has been found to be often intercepted by the emergence of an autocratic government, military administration and so on. In Western democracies, this is a development hard to expect. This is because of the fact that a democratic State there is strongly supported by a democratic society. By democratic society is meant a kind of society the autonomy of which is respected by the State and never interfered with. In other words, democracy there rests on a powerful social base. This has been possible not by way of any gracious move by a generous State but by the activity of a powerful civil society. The historical development in Western democracies has led to the growth of a powerful civil society which constantly

Notes

acts as a vigilant guard of the society against political interference in social matters. But in most of the countries of the Third World, just noted, democracy has failed or faltered just because of the weakness of civil society. For instance, the State in Pakistan from the very beginning has tried to cash in religious jingoism in order to fortify its authority, and accordingly a social environment congenial to civil society has ever eluded this country. On the contrary, in Bangladesh a powerful social movement relating to language eventually led to the growth of a viable civil society. As a result, after many trials and tribulations, a relatively strong democracy has come to stay.

The case in India is altogether different. Ever since the installation of a sovereign democratic republic on 26 January 1950, democracy in India apparently has been consistently functioning quite well. Its political structure, despite all odds, is quite intact; the constitutional rules guiding democracy have all along been faithfully followed, and India indeed has won worldwide acclaim for having been able to sustain democracy all these years. Yet all is not well with Indian democracy. Its form no doubt remains unhurt, but its normative spirit, which actually is the source of strength of a democracy, seems to be under heavy stress. This is mainly because the power holders and power seekers (i.e., political parties) who run democracy or aspire to run it have been somehow used to viewing democracy only as a form of government and not as a way of life. Hence, no wonder forgetting that democracy is a system mainly committed to the cause of the people, they tend to treat it as a forum for a wrestling bout that would decide who eventually would occupy the seat of power. In other words, least concerned about how to improve the health of democracy and how to give it wholesome sustenance, they are more interested in capturing power and holding it. Thus, Indian democracy has now turned into what may be called Machiavellian democracy.

This brief sketch of the historical development of democracy in the Third World countries leads to two conclusions about the nature of democracy. First, democracy cannot be regarded to be a success in a country if the latter has well nurtured a democratic government, routinely following the rules and norms that determine its structure. Actually, its success depends on the extent to which the politicians, the people and of course the media at work under its canopy have been able to treat it as a way of life and reflect this way of life in all their functions, attitude and behaviour. Second, to ensure the success of democracy, there must be active a powerful civil society to keep a close watch on the functioning of a democratic government, warn it about its lapses and, if necessary, launch a countrywide social movement to rouse public opinion about these lapses. Democracy may be truly sound only when these two conditions are fulfilled. This confirms that Laski in a sense was right when for the success of democracy, he strongly held a brief for the development of a pluralist society.

Notes

FORMS OF DEMOCRACY

Some of the modern theorists have viewed democracy from their respective angles and have accordingly identified different forms of democracy. Again, some have tried to classify democracy into various forms. For instance, David Held has made a fivefold classification of democracy. However, viewed in the context of contemporary realities, democracy appears to have the following forms: (a) developmental democracy, (b) participatory democracy and (c) consociational democracy.

Developmental democracy means that kind of democracy which besides functioning as a people's government intimately links itself with the task of economic development of the country. In fact, in modern times, it appears that economic development is the key concern of all democratic governments of the world. Against the backdrop of globalization and introduction of free market economy, there is now a fierce competition among the democratic countries of the world to augment the rate of their respective growth. In the developed nations where economic disparity is not too wide, the tryst of a democratic government with this growth rush causes no serious problem; at least the government is not stigmatized as actually a government for the rich. Democracy here, besides doing its routine work, keeps itself committed to the goal of faster economic growth which hardly affects the democratic ideal. But in a country like India where more than 70 per cent of wealth is concentrated at the hands of 1 per cent of people, developmental democracy is fraught with serious problem, for here meaningful development is possible only by a balanced redistribution of wealth so that the poor income group equally gets with others the share of increased wealth. But with the operation of free economy and absence of planned redistributive control, it is not possible to take the flow of wealth to the lower level. Thus, in a country like India, the developmental democracy remains a democracy for the rich and not for the poor. True, to avert this crisis Indian developmental democracy for some time in past has been following the path of what is known as 'inclusive development'. In principle, inclusive development denotes a kind of economic development that benefits everyone including those who economically lag much behind. However, in practice the Indian government, led by the idea that the fruits of economic growth must be taken even to the lowest stratum, undertakes a series of welfare programmes in order to ameliorate the conditions of the urban and rural poor. But these welfare schemes may have only a marginal effect on the eradication of poverty and distress but can hardly lift the marginalized sections of people to the level of the better off. Indeed, inclusive development by any measure can be no substitute for redistribution of wealth. Thus, in countries like India developmental democracy makes no sense unless it is backed up by equitable distribution. Hence, it is

Notes

found that Indian democracy stands foremost in producing billionaires, but about one-third of its people lie below the poverty line. Thus, it may be concluded that though developmental democracy is most needed in developing nations, the free economy they have in recent times embraced stands as a stupendous impediment against making it a success.

In ancient Athens where citizens could participate directly in the deliberative process, democracy to a large extent was participatory. Although in modern indirect democracy, marked by a representative system, citizens have little opportunity for direct participation; they no doubt can indirectly participate in the governing process. Thus, democracy by nature is somewhat participatory. However, in the last quarter of the 20th century under the theoretical initiative of some writers, C. B. Macpherson being the most vocal among them, the idea of participatory democracy as a distinct form evolved. Participatory democracy is that kind of democracy which facilitates greater participation by the citizens. Macpherson, as just noted, makes the strongest plea for participatory democracy. The idea no doubt sounds very attractive. Indeed, if modern representative democracy were based on greater participation by the people, it would really be nearer to the ideal of a people's government. But what about the possible mechanism to ensure this greater popular participation? To this question, the advocates of participatory democracy have no clear answer. Macpherson, of course, argues that if the internal structure of the party is more democratized involving greater popular participation, then party government which is an essential feature of a democratic government will by implication be more participatory. But the solution is more presumptive than real.

There are however two ways to make modern democracy more participatory. One way is to develop a very powerful civil society. If the civil society is strong enough to influence the decision-making process of a democratic government, if as a people's watchdog it exposes the lapses of the government and by creating public opinion against it forces the government to change its course of action, then surely it encourages participatory democracy, for in the ultimate analysis, civil society represents the voice of the people in an organized form. The other way is to arrest concentration of power and work for decentralization of power so that democracy is taken down to the grass roots level so much so that people at that level may directly and actively participate in the decision-making process. India's village panchayat system, introduced by the 73rd constitutional amendment of 1992, is an outstanding experiment of participatory democracy. To what extent this system in actual practice has developed a participatory democracy is a debatable question. But at least theoretically viewed, it must be treated as a prototype of participatory democracy.

Consociational democracy is related only to parliamentary democracy. Parliamentary democracy presupposes a majority rule. In this system, the party

Notes

commanding majority in the lower house of the legislature forms government that runs for a fixed term. However, it may so happen that sometimes electoral results fail to give absolute majority to any of the contesting parties. But as parliamentary system does not work without a government in charge of governance, in such a situation several parties join together to form a coalition assured of majority support in the lower house of the legislature. This is known as consociational democracy. It may also be called coalitional democracy. Consociational democracy may also come into being against an altogether different background. Sometimes, in the case of national security being threatened by war, external aggression or other exigencies, in a parliamentary democracy the ruling party together with other parties may agree to have a coalition in the form of a national government, as it happened in Britain in 1939 in the wake of the Second World War.

It cannot be denied that consociational democracy is symptomatic of the electoral weaknesses of the political contenders. It is also true that consociational form is less stable than a one-party majority rule. Further, consociational democracy is more likely in a multiparty system where chances of uneven and, sometimes, erratic distribution of votes are much higher than in a biparty system. Yet in Britain, which is the traditional home ground of parliamentary democracy and marked mainly by a biparty system, during the last one hundred years a coalition government has been at work for five times.

Depending on the timing, nature and goal of coalition, consociational democracy may be of different forms. For instance, coalition may be pre-poll and post-poll. The post-poll coalition naturally is not pre-planned. Rather a rash exercise under political and constitutional compulsions, it suffers from all the limitations of an ad hoc arrangement, including the problem of instability. Pre-poll coalition is free from these problems. Since it is planned beforehand, it approaches the electorate as a coherent body and the latter knowingly votes for the coalition. Obviously, the consociational democracy born out of it enjoys stability. Viewed in the context of their goal, coalitions may be divided into two categories—indispensable and strategic. When a large party intent on forming government anticipates that by its own political strength alone it cannot win the elections, then to serve its purpose it is led to enter into coalition with some smaller parties. This may be called indispensable coalition. Strategic coalition on the other hand is qualitatively different from indispensable coalition. Here, a large party forms coalition with smaller ones, not because it apprehends that it does not have sufficient strength to win the elections but because it takes it as a well-planned strategy to avoid division of votes going to the advantage of the opposition camp. Thus, here the only goal is to keep the opposition electorally weak. Depending on the basis of its formation, a coalition may further be classified into indiscriminate and ideological. When a coalition is based on no long-term considerations and rational criterion but is solely guided by a desperate urge

Notes

to form government, it is called an indiscriminate coalition. In this type, quantity alone is the prime consideration and not quality. That is, it is a coalition based only on a careful calculation of the required number and, accordingly, whichever party is willing to join the coalition, no matter whether at one time it had been in the enemy camp, is eagerly roped in. Obviously, the consociational democratic form born out of this type of coalition suffers from instability. Ideological coalition on the contrary is constituted by parties having at least a minimum ideological kinship. This ideological bond no doubt adds immense strength to the coalition. It may be noted that in West Bengal, a state of India, this ideological coalition enabled the Left Front government to rule the state for 34 years. Thus, all these years consociational democracy was a great success in West Bengal. It may be noted in the end that Switzerland provides an ideal example of consociational democracy. It is governed by the constitutional rule that Federal Council, which is the name of the federal government, shall be constituted by the representatives of all political parties.

CRITIQUES OF DEMOCRACY

Democracy however is not free from critiques. Ever since the development of the grand elite theory by Pareto, Mosca and Michels in the last century, the perception about democracy has undergone significant changes. Critics of democracy armed with the logic of the elite theory now argue that democracy is a government hardly by the people; it is only a government by the politically articulated few, that is, the elite. True in theory, democracy is supposed to be a government that underscores the democratic ideal of popular sovereignty. But in actual practice, people in a democracy have very little of sovereignty. They are actually sovereign only on the day or days of election. But once the government is formed in presidential or parliamentary democracy, people virtually have no role to play. Kept permanently at the receiving end, their only task is to watch the government in action and faithfully carry out its orders. Even when the government takes a hard decision having far-reaching effects on their lives, there is generally no mechanism available to seek their opinion or consult them. It may be counterclaimed that people send their representatives to the legislature, who on their behalf keep a constant check on executive excesses, and thereby subject the government to popular will. But it may be pointed out that in a presidential democracy, the president as the chief executive acts independent of the legislature and therefore representatives of the people in the legislature have actually no regulatory power over government. In a parliamentary democracy of course because of the executive accountability to the legislature, representatives of people in the legislature are substantially empowered to control the government. But as parliamentary democracy is essentially a party government, the government in this system by virtue of party support in the legislature may easily run, disregarding

Notes

the will of the people. Thus, viewed in whatever way democracy cannot dispense with the charge of being an elite government.

Another criticism democracy is subjected to is that irrespective of presidential and parliamentary form, it is a government by amateurs. Barring exceptions, the president in a presidential democracy and the Council of Ministers in a parliamentary democracy have no long and adequate experience of politics and governance. This amateurism of the executive is usually compensated by the bureaucrats who have long and uninterrupted experience and knowledge of the things to be done at the executive level. Thus, members of the executive in a democratic system are often found to depend heavily on the assistance and services rendered by the bureaucrats. This inevitably leads to bureaucratic hegemony in government. But bureaucrats are by no means representatives of the people. Further, they have no accountability to the people. Hence, this bureaucratization of democratic government makes havoc of the democratic ideal of people's sovereignty.

Democracy may mostly be freed from these limitations, if in a democracy both the government, including both the political executive and the bureaucratic executive, and the governed tend to take democracy not just as a form of government but more as a way of life, that is, if they lay greater emphasis on the values of democracy rather than on its structure. A firm commitment to these values will constantly warn the political executive and the permanent executive, that is the bureaucracy, that they have to exercise their defined power just as people's representatives and not as self-styled rulers. Similarly, it will teach the people to develop among themselves democratic culture and faithfully follow it so that they may duly discharge their responsibilities to keep democracy alive. Thus, democracy may continue its triumphant march only when it is viewed by all concerned just as a way of life.

14

CHAPTER

Political Ideology

Notes

INTRODUCTION

Political ideology is born out of a coherent political idea. Yet every idea is not ideology. Indeed in the past two millenniums and a half, there have been ideas galore in the political domain. But very few of them have earned the distinction of being an ideology. A well-organized political idea may be regarded as a political ideology only when it involves certain guiding principles and also a programme meant to implement such principles, and further, when with these it may be used as a ruling idea determining and regulating the nature and functions of a particular kind of political system. However, a political ideology does not necessarily have to be a guiding principle of a political system. What is needed is that it must have the potential to be the ruling idea behind a political system. Thus, anarchism and Gandhism have never shaped a political system. But as they have enough materials to bring into being a distinct political system, they are included in the category of political ideology.

Karl Marx, it may be noted, denied the independent and creative role of ideology. He viewed ideology as a component of the superstructure conditioned by the economic base of society. Accordingly, he regarded ideology as a means to fortify the capitalist society. Engels went one step forward by declaring ideology as a 'false consciousness'. However, Lenin subsequently freed ideology from its pejorative implications and argued for a socialist ideology that he felt would develop working-class consciousness. No wonder when a socialist political

Notes

system was installed in the Soviet Union, in some East European countries as well as in China, a socialist ideology was found to be the ruling principle guiding these systems. Today, therefore, it is noticed all over the world that behind every political system there is an ideology at work. This of course confirms the importance of ideology.

In the present world, the political ideologies that merit attention are liberalism, Marxism, fascism, anarchism and Gandhism. As pointed out above, the last two have not yet been found to be a ruling idea behind any political system. Yet for reasons stated above, they are recognized as prominent political ideologies in the modern world. Liberalism was born more than 300 years ago in the writings of John Locke, a 17th-century English political philosopher. In subsequent times, it has taken different routes under the initiative of a good many thinkers. However, its essence has remained unchanged, and even in the present century it has won the distinction of being the most accepted and dominant political ideology. Marxism is a 19th-century ideology coming out of the ideas of Marx and Engels, though in the 20th century it underwent important changes by virtue of ideas presented in the 20th century by Lenin, Gramsci, Stalin and Mao Zedong. But with the collapse of the socialist states, nearly all over the world, the importance of Marxism as an ideology is now at a low ebb. Fascism evolved in Mussolini's Italy in the 20th century. The distinctiveness of this ideology is that its advocates gave greater emphasis on application than on ideation. Indeed, in the 20th-century Italy, the fascist state was first established and then followed the fascist ideology to support it. With the end of the Second World War, fascism had its natural death. Anarchism as an ideology flourished in the early 19th century. Although it created a great stir in the contemporary world, gradually it lost its edge. While all these ideologies developed in the Western world, Gandhism is an ideological product of India. The very characteristic that distinguishes Gandhism from all other ideologies is its emphasis on the question of morality. Indeed, it is the mixture of politics and morals that has made Gandhism a unique ideology in the world.

LIBERALISM

Liberalism, as noted earlier, is the oldest political ideology of the world. As it is a dynamic ideology, at different historical phases it has enriched its content and changed its route under the influence of various ideas and incidents. Obviously, myriad factors have been at work behind its development.

The first of these was no doubt the Reformation movement of the 16th century, launched by Martin Luther in a small town of Germany. This movement raised a strong protest against the then absolute authority of the Church of Rome

Notes

and argued that religion was personal and not institutional; that is, every Christian individual had the freedom to interpret the Bible applying his own judgement without waiting for the dictate of the Church in this regard. Thus, though the Reformation was primarily a religious movement, it involved two political premises in that no institutional authority was final and that an individual had the freedom to interpret and explain in the light of his own judgement. Thus, the Reformation set the perspective for liberalism, for the essence of liberalism is that authority by nature is limited and that freedom of the individual is the most prized possession.

The Glorious Revolution of England of 1688 introduced for the first time in the country constitutional monarchy, which in actual practice limited the authority of the king. Obviously, liberalism with its characteristic of limited authority was much inspired by this revolution. Two years after, Locke brought out his famous work *Two Treatises of Government.* In the second part of this work, Locke laid the theoretical foundation of liberalism by delineating in it the main characteristics of liberalism. No wonder Locke is regarded as the father of Western liberal ideology.

The American Revolution of 1776 and the French Revolution of 1789 are also regarded as important sources of liberalism, for these two revolutions were essentially a struggle for human freedom which is the avowed goal of liberalism. The 18th-century European Enlightenment that upheld reason as the main determining principle of life may also be regarded as a source of liberalism which has developed with reason as its base. Further, against the backdrop of English Industrial Revolution liberalism in the 19th century became a very powerful ideology. Accordingly, no one disputes the Industrial Revolution as the veritable source of liberalism.

Liberalism, it may be noted, has attained the status of a political ideology because it is not just a theoretical doctrine but is what may be given effect to in practice. Indeed, applied in practice it has given birth to democratic political system. However, liberalism is not merely confined to politics. It also has an economic dimension. In fact, economic liberalism has been experimented at different times in the past and even today, the experiment is continuing. Liberalism is the only ideology that recognizes the importance of authority and at the same time prioritizes rights, freedom and dignity of the individual. In fact, one of the main goals of liberalism is to effect reconciliation of the authority of the State with freedom of the individual. The advocates of liberalism are of the opinion that property is the means to develop the personality of the individual and hence serves as a root of the development of human civilization. Liberalism is thus committed to the system of private property. One of the striking features of liberalism, it may be added, is its emphasis on a clear distinction between State and society. This has led it to underscore the autonomy of society and not to

Notes

interpret, unlike Marxism, the nature of the State in terms of its social base. Again, unlike Marxism, liberalism does not believe in a radical and revolutionary change. It reposes faith on gradual and peaceful change. In other words, it is reformist and not revolutionary.

The ideas on the basis of which liberalism as an ideology has grown are as follows. First, despite the authority of the State the individual is ordained to submit to, he has his own autonomous area free from interference by the State. It is in this area that the individual is sovereign. Second, freedom of the individual is his valued treasure which no one can violate, not even the powerful State. Third, as an independent entity, the individual has certain fundamental (or what Locke identifies as natural) rights, which the State cannot deny nor can interfere with. It is these rights that help the individual maintain his freedom even within the framework of political control. Fourth, the State no doubt is armed with coercive power. But in the ultimate analysis, the source of the power of the State is individual's voluntary consent. In the context of this individual consent, the State remains ever accountable to the individual. Fifth, what is born out of these ideas is that the authority of the State over the individual is not absolute and unlimited. The State enjoys limited authority, as its main responsibility is to protect the rights of the individual and not to affect his autonomy. In case the State fails to discharge this responsibility, the individual is entitled to resist those who rule. Sixth, as indicated earlier liberalism is based on the idea that the State and society are different from each other. Since society enjoys autonomy, the individual has a double identity. On the one hand, he is a political animal, that is a citizen of a State. On the other, he is a social animal committed to the cause of society. This proves that despite political control the individual has an autonomous area where he is free from political control and coercion.

Over the years, liberalism is found to have assumed different forms. These are classical liberalism, economic liberalism, individualist liberalism, neoliberalism, pluralist liberalism, libertarianism and communitarianism.

John Locke in his *Two Treatises of Government* initiated what is known as classical liberalism. He earmarked an autonomous area of the individual and argued that in this autonomous sphere, the individual freely enjoys his right to life, freedom and property, which the State cannot interfere with in any way. The State has to exercise its power subject to the condition that it will accept responsibility to protect these rights. Hence, the State has limited authority. On the other hand, the source of the power of the State is decidedly the individual, for since the individual consents to submit to the power of the State, the latter is able to exercise its power. During more than 300 years following Locke, there no doubt have been very many changes in the nature and form of liberalism. But what was said by Locke has primarily been accepted in all liberal quarters.

Notes

Economic liberalism was parented by Adam Smith in his work *The Wealth of Nations* published in 1776. His main argument was that one of the surest ways to augment national wealth was to let the individual absolutely unregulated in his economic enterprises. This is how at the theoretical level was born a fierce economic individualism which is known in history as laissez faire. Taking cue from Adam Smith's economic liberalism was developed individualist liberalism under the aegis of Jeremy Bentham and John Stuart Mill, two great utilitarians. Bentham in his *A Manual of Political Economy* argued in favour of minimizing state control. On the other hand, Mill in his *On Liberty* divided the individual life into self-regarding sphere and other-regarding sphere, and claimed that in his self-regarding sphere, the State had no right to interfere as in this sphere the individual was fully sovereign over his body and mind. About the same time, with the aid of the Darwinian theory, Herbert Spencer transformed individualist liberalism into an extreme opposition to the State. He viewed submission to State control as a kind of slavery and felt that an unabated State control would finally invite totalitarianism.

In the 1870s, a trend set in to give a new dimension to liberalism by tempering its individualist ferocity. The trend was initiated by T. H. Green, a noted English idealist philosopher. The thesis he upheld was that State control, in no way, is antithetic to the freedom of the individual. On the contrary, it is contributory and complementary to it. This kind of liberalism introduced by Green, by ending the tradition of blind opposition to the State, has come to be known as neoliberalism. This was further expanded by J. M. Keynes in the 1930s and by William Beveridge in the 1940s. Keynes was a strong critic of the 18th-century economic individualism. His point was that State control of the economy is not unwarranted as it adds power and prosperity to a liberal society. Beveridge on the other hand was of the opinion that one of the main duties of a liberal State is to ensure social security to its citizens. However, this duty calls for State interference in the life of the individual.

A 20th-century theoretical development, pluralist liberalism was initiated by Harold Laski. He believed that freedom of the individual, a cherished ideal of liberalism, best flourishes in a federal society, a society marked by autonomous activities of various social groups. In the same vein, authors such as Raymond Aron, S. M. Lipset, Robert Dahl and David Truman held that to what extent the individual enjoys freedom is determined by how much and how frequently he actively participates in the functions of voluntary social organizations. That is, freedom of the individual depends on the autonomy of social organizations. The more these social organizations would enjoy freedom, freer would be the society which alone would bring in an environment congenial to the protection of individual freedom.

In the post-Second World War West, the liberal ideology underwent a turning point. Liberal theorists such as W. G. Sumner, C. Menger, Isaiah Berlin, F. A.

Notes

Hayek and Robert Nozick revived the individualist liberal tradition of the past, and this so-called old wine in a new bottle came to be known as libertarianism. Notwithstanding their varying arguments, the central point they all share is that man is an animal with a definitive purpose. But this purpose is hardly fulfilled unless men are completely free in the exercise of their choices and in their activities. Hence, what is required is minimal State interference. This also, according to them, calls for an economic system characterized by free competitive market in the context of which the State's only task is to maintain the system, ensure social justice and look after defence, and nothing else.

Libertarianism, after its birth, however was subjected to severe criticism. Its critics discredited it by viewing it as a retrograde step to take shelter in the past tradition that hardly fits in with modern needs. However, it is a historical irony that in the 21st century, with globalization and free market economy having been almost universally accepted across the world, libertarianism freed from all stigma stands triumphant.

It may be added that in the 20th century, as a reaction to libertarianism emerged a new brand of liberalism known as communitarianism. Theorists such as Michael Oakeshott, Hannah Arendt, Alasdair MacIntyre, Michael Sandel, Charles Taylor and Daniel Bell were its advocates. Despite their argumentative differences, what they agree on is that without a communitarian perspective, freedom and rights of the individual do not attain sustainability. That is, an individual's freedom does not mean liberty from all liability. An individual to enjoy freedom must accept his liability and commitment to community or society. In other words, an individual is free only as a social animal. The idea however is not unique. Long before the communitarians, T. H. Green, in his liberal idea, stressed on this point. In fact, taking cue from Hegel (though he never acknowledged his debt to Hegel on that score), he held that man is free only in a social perspective. Hence, it is not inappropriate to consider communitarianism as basically a restatement of Green's neoliberalism.

Although liberal ideology over times has taken various forms, its essence, of course, remains the same. That eternally valid essence is that for the fulfilment of possibilities inherent in himself, man needs freedom and that this freedom best flourishes in a free society. This free society, however, does not mean a completely unregulated society. Indeed, liberalism accepts the necessity of both social and political control. However, what it underscores is that this control must be contributory to the development of a person's self and realization of his inherent possibilities. Otherwise control will curb freedom. This reconciliation of freedom and control is the eternal message of liberalism.

It is true that liberalism gives greater emphasis on freedom than on equality. This has been a point of criticism against it. Critics further point out that the political system, based on liberal ideology, encourages economic enterprises

Notes

under private ownership and accordingly private profit earners thrive on exploitation of the working class. This, in effect, amounts to denial of individual freedom and dignity. In view of this, critics of liberalism like John Dunn tend to look down on liberalism as 'a tasteless exercise in vanity and selfdeception'. But this is rather an unkind assessment. After all, it appears that all modern liberal States, despite their libertarian overtones, are keen on ensuring redistributive justice for their citizens by taking to various socially constructive measures. It may further be said that the critics of liberalism have so far not been able to offer a viable alternative to it. The only strong challenge that came from Marxism and continued for sometime is now all over. Today, only the liberal ideology rules the world, having no other ideological substitute to shake its foundation. Hence, there is no other option than to hail liberalism as the best possible ideology of the world.

ANARCHISM

Anarchism is a negative political ideology. It seeks to deny and destroy but hardly constructs. Actually, it presupposes defiance of all institutional authority but does not suggest what should replace it. It is essentially a theoretical discourse supported by no programme of action. Hence, it is an ideology by default.

English Industrial Revolution led to striking capitalist development in the 19th-century England. As a result, by the middle of the 19th century, England became the wealthiest nation of the world and by virtue of massive development of its factory system, it came to be known as the 'workshop of the world'. However, in the absence of any mechanism for redistribution of wealth, the augmented national wealth totally went to the capitalist class, leaving the working class in abject sufferings. Eventually, this social divide became so acute that Disraeli in his 'two-nation' theory regretted that his contemporary country had been divided into two nations—the rich and the poor. At one point, the untold misery of the poor working class led them to view machines as the root of all trouble. Accordingly, they unitedly began wrecking machines, which is known in history as the Luddite movement. The authority took no time to crush the movement. The failure of this movement, it may be added, was inevitable, for it was a misdirected movement in that the Luddites failed to comprehend that it was not the machine but the social system generated by the Industrial Revolution that was responsible for all the trouble they were facing. Interestingly, the misconceived target of attack of the Luddites was carried on theoretically by the anarchists.

William Godwin is generally regarded as the father of anarchism, though he himself never claimed that he was an anarchist. In his *Enquiry Concerning Political Justice*, his central argument is that man is not bound to do anything that offends his independent power of judgement. He also argued that the unjust economic system that develops under the indulgence of the coercive state hinders man's independent self-development and moral behaviour. Unless man is freed from this system, he cannot act rationally and justly. Accordingly, in his opinion, the State and the private property system encourage social and moral evil. This is how Godwin at least indirectly subscribes to anarchism. In his book *What Is Property*, Pierre-Joseph Proudhon however declared himself as an anarchist. He was an anarchist in that he completely opposed the authority of the State. In *The General Idea of the Revolution in the Nineteenth Century*, he argued that to obey the authority of the State is to surrender to the commands of those who have neither right nor prudence or qualities to issue this command. Viewing in this light, he regarded the French Revolution as no revolution at all. To him, revolution signifies a scenario with 'no authority, no government, not even popular'. On the other hand, he stigmatized property as theft. Despite this drastic condemnation however he could not totally reject the system of property. In fact, he wanted to introduce a new economic system which be branded as 'mutualism'. According to him, this mutualism will be a system free from all exploitation by tax collectors, usurers and the middlemen in business. It will be a state of things where individuals and groups will carry on business by virtue of free bargaining among themselves and each will be ready to render services to others. But there will be no scope for profiteering or exploitation. Social interaction will be voluntary, bringing in benefits and harmonious relations to all in a condition free from State control and interference. This system of mutualism, Proudhon further argues, will be such that individuals or groups engaged in productive enterprises may draw their necessary finance from cooperative banks at a very little interest or no interest at all. According to him, this cooperative banking system introduced on a large scale will stop private capital earning profit and, as a result, all coercive institutions will be unnecessary. Proudhon himself calls this idea as positive anarchism. It is with this anarchist ideology, it may be mentioned, that Proudhon threw Marx to a challenge that eventually led to the split of the International Labour Movement. The thread left by Proudhon was later picked up by Bakunin and Kropotkin to continue tirade against the Marxist ideology.

Bakunin begins his anarchism with the aid of his self-formulated theory of evolution. According to him, the lowest historical phase of the evolution of man was virtually an era of brutes wherefrom through evolutionary process came the higher phase with true human beings. But he considers the State, religion and private property as natural institutions growing in the lower phase, and hence he argues that in the higher phase their extinction is inevitable. Armed with this argument, Bakunin rejects all political control. In his opinion, the State apparatus even when it is democratic implies autocracy, for the ignorant and inexperienced people are always helpless in the face of the strategy of the economically powerful class which, to serve its interest, uses the State power whatever be its

Notes

form. Thus, Bakunin opposes the State on economic grounds. According to him, the system of private ownership of the means of production keeps the people in subordination to the owners of capital. On the other hand, the State is based on the system of private property and is committed to perpetuate this system. Naturally, the most important task of the State is to support and protect exploitation of the working class by the property owners. This is why Bakunin opposes the State. On moral grounds also, Bakunin opposes the State and private property. He argues that the State always forces those under its rule to do work for it. But compulsion makes no room for moral and intellectual development, and, hence, it leads to moral degradation of the governed. On the other hand, moral degeneration also befalls those who run the State, for as participants in power they begin regarding themselves as superior people, though they have little worth. Thus, they actually turn into morally inferior people, though they enjoy political power. Further, Bakunin continues, the private property system leaves the working people in bondage. They have to work hard with least scope for mobility. On the contrary, the propertied minority get ample financial comfort and have enough opportunity before them for self-development. So Bakunin adjudges private property as immoral. Besides, religion too is immoral to Bakunin. Because according to him religion always lends support to the immoral authority of the economically and politically ruling class.

Kropotkin, another Russian anarchist like Bakunin, begins with a theory of evolution which is poles apart from that of Darwin. The key to Darwinian evolution is conflict or struggle. Kropotkin's evolution on the contrary is based on cooperation. According to him, following the process of evolution only those finally survive who, in pursuance of the rule of cooperation, are able to adjust themselves with the environment. On the other hand, those who fail to survive, that is, those who are lost, rely on competition and not on cooperation. The rule of mutual cooperation, Kropotkin continues, ushers in equality, justice and social harmony. Therefore, the key principle of social progress is that what is done in case of one must be done in case of the other. However, this basic law of progress is thwarted by the State and private property and also by religious authority that supports political oppression and economic privilege. Kropotkin detests the State because it destroys the tendency of man to cooperate. The State stabilizes its authority on the basis of the false assumption that men by nature are competitive and hence anti-social. In this perspective, the State to maintain order in society deems it necessary to exercise coercion and control. But Kropotkin believes that man's life went on for long without a State. Only when the oppressor and the oppressed classes had emerged, the State with its laws came into being to serve as a supportive agency of social exploitation. Naturally, according to Kropotkin the State has no positive role in removing the distress and sufferings of people. It has never tried to protect industrial workers from capitalist exploitation and guard the peasantry against the exploitation by landowners. Hence, freedom of speech, freedom of press, personal freedom and so on are all meaningless, as they hardly may be exercised against the economically privileged class. This situation remains unchanged even with a change in the form of the State. Thus, when monarchy marked by absolute personal sovereignty was transformed into a democratic system embracing popular sovereignty, there was hardly any change in the nature of the State. Kropotkin thus attacks not only the State but also the system of private property. To him, property is an evil, for with its aid the minority enjoys the benefits accruing from hard mental and manual labour rendered by thousands of people for ages. Naturally, according to Kropotkin a property owner is not in the right to claim that property is just his to the exclusion of others. Further, to focus the evil effect of property on social life, Kropotkin argues, the property system has caused unemployment and hardship to a huge number of people, left the peasantry in a great amount of rural debt, obstructed the natural development of children and on the contrary brought to the wealthy minority a life of luxury, extravagance, indolence and attachment to crude pleasure. Hence, there is the need to destroy the State and private property system.

The idea underlying the anarchist ideology is the primacy of the individual. In that sense, anarchism may be said to have derived its inspiration from the sophist aphorism that 'man is the measure of all things'. Like the sophist philosophers of ancient Greece, the anarchists are convinced that a totally free individual with his independent power of judgement may decide what is good for him and the society he lives in. This is why they oppose the State which in their view symbolizes control and coercion. They are also against property and religion which they view as the handmaid of the State. To them, revolution presupposes dissolution of all authority and laws. This conviction led Kropotkin to consider the Bolshevik Revolution as a misguided movement. His comment on it was that the Bolshevik attempt to construct a communist republic with the aid of centralized State communism and party dictatorship must ultimately prove to be a futile historical exercise. Thus, anarchists were at loggerheads with the Marxists.

It was natural for the anarchists with their burning faith on the moral autonomy of the individual to take this position. But what was left unanswered in their ideology was the question how society would run with the destruction of all institutional authority. The anarchists might argue in defence of their position that mutualism underscored by Proudhon or cooperation highlighted by Kropotkin would be the ruling principle running the society. But what they failed to realize is that this ruling principle to be given effect to definitely needs a mechanism and this is why what is required is an institutional framework. Anarchism gives no importance and attention to this institutional framework. Thus, anarchism to the end remained a utopia that could not be used as an ideology governing a political system. That is why in the realm of political ideologies, it remains an idea that may provoke only excitement but draws only an academic interest and nothing else.

Notes

MARXISM

Marxism, primarily developed by Marx and Engels in the 19th century, has all the merit for being a distinctive political ideology, for it is based on a logically developed coherent idea leaving no question unanswered and has the worth to be the guiding ideology of a political system. In fact, for many decades it has helped building a viable and powerful political system in nearly one-third of the world. Further, no other political ideology except Gandhism is based on a comprehensive philosophy of life and the world than that of Marx. For instance, Locke, who laid the foundation of liberal ideology, initiated the philosophy of empiricism. Yet his empiricism is not directly linked with his liberalism. On the other hand, the two philosophical pillars on which stands the entire edifice of Marxist ideology are the philosophy of dialectical materialism and historical materialism. This is what makes Marxism a unique ideology.

Although unique and highly original, Marxism derives some of its elements from various sources. The primary source is of course the philosophy of Hegel. Marx is much indebted to dialectics which determines Hegel's philosophical approach. However, he turns it upside down in that while Hegelian dialectics emphasizes ideas, Marx focuses material forces as the centre of his dialectics. Second, the German philosopher Feuerbach was also a source. Although Marx mostly opposed him and in fact produced an important part of his doctrine in 1845 by way of his disagreement with Feuerbach, he indeed was inspired by Feuerbach's thesis that philosophy may well assist in solving the concrete problems of man. Besides, Feuerbach's materialist critique of religion was also a source of Marxian materialism. The third source was classical English economy led by David Ricardo. The classical English economists for the first time theoretically proved that labour is the source of any commodity produced and that the value of a commodity is determined by this labour. This no doubt inspired Marx's famous theory of surplus value. Fourth, the French socialism that evolved prior to the emergence of Marxism also provided a starting point to Marx. For instance, in the beginning of the 19th century, the French socialist Saint Simon held the view that property relations determine the character of a society. This view, as we shall see later, was very much followed in Marx's historical materialism. On the other hand, in the middle of the 19th century French socialist Louis Auguste Blanqui developed a structure of proletarian rule which was well utilized by Marx. About the same time, another French socialist Louis Blanc formulated the principle, 'from each one according to his ability, to each one according to his needs'. This was used by Marx as the basic rule governing the new society he visualized.

The Marxian ideology is essentially an ideology of change. Marx decided to use this ideology as an instrument to bring in a radical change of the world.

Notes

Indeed, all along he was led by the conviction that 'the philosophers have only interpreted the world in various ways, the point however is to change it'. In order to logically justify the inevitability of this change, Marx enunciated a philosophy which is known as dialectical materialism. The entire structure of Marxian ideology is based on this philosophy. Marx's dialectical materialism comprises several premises. First, the world is entirely a world of matter. Second, every component of this world is not an isolated entity. It is integrally related to the other and is influenced by the other. That is, each material influences the other and is influenced by it. Thus, the material world is interrelated. Third, matter by nature is in a flux. Hence, changeability represents the very character of the material world. Accordingly, there is a constant change in every matter and so in this world there is nothing like perpetual or eternal. Fourth, this change is always progressive; that is, it takes the world to move forward and not backward. Further, this change is not only quantitative but also qualitative. That is, there is continuous change in every matter and this change takes it to a higher and a better position. Fifth, no external force causes this change. The matter that undergoes change has the seed of change within itself. Every matter comprises two elements—positive and negative. It is the incompatibility and conflict between these two elements that forces qualitative and progressive change of the matter. Further, as this change comes about through conflict and struggle, it never comes in a straight line nor is it smooth. This means that every qualitative and progressive change of the world arrives by way of struggle and resistance, that is, revolution. This dialectical materialism, obviously, provides a logical and philosophical support to the Marxian ideology of change. To cite a conclusive historical evidence of the validity of this doctrine of change, Marx makes a thorough enquiry of history. Or, it may be said, he applies his philosophy of dialectical materialism on the plane of history in order to interpret it in the light of the former. This interpretation is known as historical materialism.

Marx introduces his historical materialism relying on several premises. First, true to his dialectical materialism, he views history as a movement of matter; that is, he believes in the materialist interpretation of history. Second, as dialectical materialism denies the isolated existence of anything, to Marx history is not a sum total of isolated events but with interrelation of its different phases it is a continuous process. Obviously then history moves according to a definite law. Third, history is not a history of the individuals; it is a history of the people, that is of the society. Fourth, this history of society is reflected in the material conditions of the life of society. Fifth, since the material conditions of life cannot go on without production, the mode of production prevailing in a society serves as the basis of the material conditions of life. Last, production is by nature social, for a single individual cannot produce a thing, it invariably requires a collective effort.

With these premises in the backdrop, Marx argues that social production involves two things—one, forces of production, and the other, relations of

Notes

production. For production are required the means of production such as raw materials, machines, and a particular place. However, these means of production cannot by themselves produce. Production is possible only when a group of people by applying their intelligence and experience properly use the means of production. This group of people together with the means of production represents what Marx calls forces of production. On the other hand, as the people engaged in production work together, they naturally develop simple human relations among themselves. For instance, in primitive society where forces of production were much undeveloped, that is, when with things like mainly stones men were used to collective hunting and do everything together for collecting the means of livelihood, relations among them were much simple and there was no division of labour. But with the invention of metal and the making of weapon out of it, some people who made such weapons put an end to collective hunting. They began hunting with their weapons and managed to allocate other jobs to the rest of the people. That is, there came about private ownership of the means of production and along with that division of labour. This means that complex property relations now replaced simple human relations. In his historical materialism, Marx identifies these complex property relations as relations of production.

The mode of production characterized by these relations of production presupposes the economic base of society. According to the character of this economic base grows on it the superstructure. The superstructure includes all social and political institutions as well as ideas. Hence, it is the mode of production that conditions the character of society. However, as the mode of production is the only means to understand the nature of a society, it also accounts for social change. At a certain stage of social development, as a natural process, forces of production are more socialized (as production by nature requires more men, more space and a larger number of machines). But there comes no corresponding change in the relations of production with private ownership of the means of production remaining intact. Thus, there develops a basic contradiction between the forces of production and the relations of production.

Whenever this contradiction between the forces of production and the relations of production intensifies, it permanently blocks the further development of production, that is, of society. In order to remove this contradiction, it becomes urgent to bring a revolutionary change in the mode of production, that is, in the nature of society. The society undergoes radical change this way.

A part of Marx's historical materialism is his theory of classes and class struggle. According to Marx, since there were no property relations in primitive society, there was no scope for the emergence of propertied and non-propertied classes with mutually antagonistic interests. Hence, the primitive society was a classless society. But as all societies subsequent to the primitive society were

Notes

characterized by property relations, the system of private ownership of the means of production continued unabated in them. Accordingly, all societies after the primitive society have been class societies because it is in the context of relation to the means of production that various groups of people come to be known as classes. In this class society, the class which owns the means of production establishes dominance by virtue of its private ownership. It does not have to give any labour in production; that is, it is not a producing class. But as it is the owning class, it plays the role of organizer in production and in this capacity it has in its possession most of the wealth produced. On the other hand, the non-owning class gives all its labour in production. But people belonging to this class are only workers and not organizers. Accordingly, they get only a small part of the wealth generated and have to submit to the dominance of the owning class. Thus, the owning class enjoys dominance in the mode of production. They are also the dominant force in the society growing on the base of this mode of production. That is, they become the ruling class in society. It is further claimed in historical materialism that the antagonistic relations between the owning class and the non-owning class inevitably put them in class struggle.

The owning class struggles in order to perpetuate its dominance and its possession of the largest share of wealth by exploiting the non-owning class—the working class. The working class on the other hand struggles to liberate itself from its subjugation to and exploitation by the owning class.

Sometimes however, there may be a conflict between the methods of exploitation of two exploiting classes. Here too, the conflict assumes the form of class struggle. Whenever this class struggle between exploiters and the exploited or between two exploiting classes takes an intensive form, there comes about a revolutionary change of society. Thus, 'the history of all hitherto existing society is the history of class struggles' and further the root of revolution lies in class struggle.

Marxism adds that following the laws of history as determined by historical materialism, there have been various forms of society, each more progressive than the earlier one, leading finally to the development of capitalist society. The capitalist society is of course more progressive than the feudal society preceding it. However, with no change in private ownership of means of production, it is also an exploitative society marked by oppression and exploitation of the working class. But with increasing socialization of the forces of production with no corresponding change in property relations, the capitalist society is entangled in a contradiction. When this contradiction is intensified, it stalls the further development of capitalism. The only way to get out of this crisis is to ensure socialization of the means of production, the primary step of which is proletarian revolution by which the proletarian class wrests power from the capitalist class and proletarian rule is established in the form of dictatorship of the proletariat.

Under the aegis of proletarian dictatorship, the process of constructing socialism is set in motion by means of planned production. When this process reaches its final stage, there is abundant production in society with the fullest socialization of the means of production. At this stage, the principle of distribution of wealth will be: 'from each according to his ability, to each according to his needs'. This means that there will be true equality among the people, classes will be abolished, social exploitation will be a thing of the past and the State as an instrument of this exploitation will wither away, that is, will die a natural death. Thus will emerge a communist society.

Marxism is essentially a quest for the freedom of man. But its distinctiveness lies in that it continues this quest in a far wider field. For instance, liberalism also symbolizes a search for freedom. However, it views freedom as liberation from the control of the coercive State and finally reaches the conclusion that real freedom comes out of a reconciliation between liberty of the individual and authority of the State. But Marxism keeps off this conciliatory approach. True, it detests the State as a coercive machinery but does not believe that freedom is possible by tempering the intensity of this coercion by way of somehow making the State contributory to the freedom of the individual. On the contrary, it goes beyond the State and focuses attention on the social system that supports it. It further adds that so long as property relations continue, the propertied class will dominate and rule the society and consequently the State, exploiting and oppressing the non-propertied classes and obviously denying them freedom. Hence, the only way to achieve freedom is to bring about a revolutionary change in social conditions where the process of socialization of the means of production begins and when finally with conscious and persistent efforts this process reaches the stage of its final fulfilment, there will be no class, let alone the aggressively exploiting ruling class, obviously no State, and the fullest freedom will finally bloom. It is in this context that Marxism has earned the distinction of being the only revolutionary ideology of the world.

Of all the ideologies, Marxism no doubt is the most organized one. It is systematically developed maintaining a perfect logical sequence. It is based on a philosophy free from all metaphysical elements. It is a philosophy that lays its entire emphasis on matter, taking nothing as permanent. That is, like a true scientist, Marx views matter as liable to constant change. On the other hand, the laws of history discovered by Marx are put to a test on the plane of history and are found to be amply proved by the historical facts of social development. Indeed, discovery of the laws of history is one of the important achievements of Marxism. As pointed out earlier, Marxism not only offers a set of coherent ideas but also includes a programme of action, mostly drawn up by Lenin much after Marx and Engels. That is why it served as a ruling principle of political systems in nearly one-third of the world for more than 70 years.

Notes

Yet Marxism is regarded today as a failed ideology. The political systems it nourished eventually collapsed like a pack of cards. There are enough reasons for this failure. Indeed, in the socialist systems emerging under the inspiration of Marxist ideology, there was no evidence of gradual weakening of the State, preparing the stage for its withering away finally. On the contrary, in these systems with the aid of over-bureaucratism the State went on getting stronger and stronger. Further, the leaders of the socialist systems, particularly Stalin, applied brutal force to get people's acceptance of their authority. What was actually needed was to give a serious attempt to generate a value system in favour of the system, that is, to produce a socialist culture. But neither Marx and Engels nor Lenin gave any importance to it. In the 1930s, Gramsci no doubt dropped a hint to that effect. But it was ignored by the so-called Marxist activists. Again, Marx and Engels and also their followers could not foresee the fantastic technological revolution of the modern age. Against the backdrop of this revolution and also the invention of nuclear arms, the class struggle has now lost much of its relevance and the States have become extremely powerful. This has largely tamed the fire of Marxism as an ideology.

FASCISM

Fascism, a 20th-century product, is a disgraced ideology. In the modern world, except a handful of erratic individuals no one else subscribes to this ideology. However, even in our times, whenever a democratic system because of the high-handedness of those who run it goes wayward, sometimes some of the signs of fascism are found to be manifest in it. The distinctiveness that differentiates fascism from other ideologies is that while all other ideologies serve as the ruling principle of a political system or at least have the potentiality to do so, fascism represents just the reverse. That is, it is not that fascism first evolved as a set of ideas and then led to the development of a system.

On the contrary, the fascist state evolved first and then in support of it, fascist ideology was developed. No wonder Benito Mussolini, known in history as the first architect of a fascist State, did not mince his words that he believed in action and not talk. Yet under the aegis of Mussolini, the fascist master, Italian intellectuals such as Alfredo Rocco and Giovanni Gentile did their best to give a shape to fascist ideology.

These thinkers who laid the foundation of fascism did not express their debt to any source. Yet it is possible to identify certain theoretical roots influencing fascism. The first of such sources was, no doubt, the German philosopher Nietzsche, who throughout put primacy on emotion than on reason. The emotion-oriented fascism clearly bears the influence of Nietzsche.

Notes

Further, Nietzsche's great trust on a superman gifted with extraordinary qualities directly inspired fascism to establish the supreme fascist leader as the saviour of mankind. On the other hand, one of the strategies of fascist ideologues was to influence people by a clever use of myths. This is where Sorel's idea of utilization of myth came to their aid. Further, Herder's theorization of nation was another source of inspiration to the fascists.

Fascism centres round the glorification of nation. In fact, nation is the kernel of fascist ideology. The fascists argue that nation is more important than the individual, for a nation which is pure is the most organized and powerful having the highest moral qualities and representing an absolute truth. Nation is more important than the individual for the further reason that with its own characteristics, culture and interests, it represents a 'higher personality'. However, the fascists point out that in the past or in their contemporary times, this kind of nation has hardly grown. Thus, on the one hand democracy with its majority rule has done a great blunder in this respect by identifying the majority of people as nation. On the other hand, socialism with its focus on economic classes has failed to grasp the real identity of nation.

According to fascism, a nation is known not by number but by qualitative excellence. Whenever with its racial uniformity and superiority, a particular group of people is able to establish its distinctiveness on the basis of its linguistic, customary and religious unity, it comes to be known as nation. A nation thus emerged attains super personality. Naturally, in the face of this nation the individual pales into insignificance. That is, for the sake of moral necessity of national interest, individual interest is to be done away with. Further, people have no role in safeguarding the national identity. It is by the will and conscience of a few individuals or just a single person that it is possible to keep alive this national identity. However, it is not enough to protect this nation with its moral identity. What is required more is to increase its strength. For this, the nation needs to be expanded which calls for extension of the territorial boundaries of a nation. This leads to the argument that the only way to protect national interest is to establish imperialism by means of war. This is why fascism presents itself as an apotheosis of militarism and imperialism. No wonder Mussolini, the ill-reputed zealot of fascism, viewed war as the best means to heighten human energy and argued that those who bravely face war earn nobility in their character.

On the basis of this aggressive nationalism, fascism determines the relation between the nation and the State. The traditional liberal view is that nation has had an important contribution behind the emergence of the State. The argument is that nation first had become quite strong and the State followed thereafter. The Western political history, it may be added, vindicates this argument.

Notes

Fascism holds just the contrary view. The fascists aver that it is not the nation that creates the State; rather, the State creates the nation. They are of the opinion that only the active national consciousness serves as a basis for the making of a nation, and it is only the State with its strong political will that may generate this consciousness. Thus, the State is the maker of the nation. Hence, the more the State is powerful, the stronger is the nation. Thus, according to Mussolini, the State is 'an ethical reality' to the advancement and increasing empowerment of which there should be no bar. Thus, fascism is in favour of an omnipotent State which overpowers the individual. Fascism minimizes the importance of the individual on the basis of the argument that as the individual has no separate identity apart from the national identity, the autonomy of the individual lies in the autonomy of nation. Again, as the State protects the identity and autonomy of the nation, the individual has no right against the State. In fact, armed with this argument, the fascists discard the liberal ideal of freedom, equality and fraternity. Besides, fascism makes it clear that the individual must accept that the person or the group of persons who run the State are above all. That is, fascism urges the individual to submit to rigid hierarchy. Further, fascism replaces the democratic slogan of freedom, equality and fraternity by that of 'responsibility, discipline and hierarchy', as it believes that these three virtues together take the individual to the higher and nobler ideal that encourages him to participate effectively in national life. This reveals that fascism denies autonomy and dignity of the individual and forces him to surrender totally to the State viewed as the sentinel and guardian of the nation.

But what would be the nature of this State? To give an answer to this question, fascism begins with a dismissal of both liberalism and socialism, that is, the popular rule of a democratic State and the proletarian rule of the socialist State. It replaces them by a new kind of State known as the 'corporate State' in the fascist circle. It may be mentioned that this corporate State was not merely confined to the realm of ideas. In fact, to give it a concrete shape the Corporation Act was enacted in Italy in 1934. The corporate State that developed in Italy was based on two premises. First, people are incapable of comprehending what nation, State and politics denote. Therefore, they would keep off the province of politics. The supreme leader and a few of his associates alone have this capability. So they only would be the decision-maker in the State and final arbiter of politics. Second, people, though made inactive in matters of politics, would of course be much active in their respective professions so that the economic progress of the nation continues unabated.

The chief characteristics of the fascist corporate State are as follows: First, at the top of the omnipotent State based on a one-party system, one or a few persons with extraordinary qualities would run governance. They would have a monopoly right to rule as they are the worthiest in this regard. Second, since

Notes

an individual is incapable of active participation in politics, he would not be treated as a political animal and hence he would have no concern for his political right, though it would be his primary duty to give unconditional allegiance to the elite ruler. However, he would be recognized as a member of a social or economic group. This would be his only identity which he would gladly accept and sincerely would do his assigned job in the interest of the welfare of the nation. Third, control by the State would not merely be political but economic as well. That is, the State would control the capitalists and also the labourers. In fact, both production and distribution would remain under the control of the State. Fourth, the corporate State would leave the private property system unaffected as it is contributory to the smooth going of production. However, it is to be seen that the private property system does not go against the national interest. This is why the State would have total control over production and distribution. That is, the State would have the right to regulate the entire economic system in the national interest. Fifth, in order to make this system of control much active and very powerful, there shall be separate forums for owners and workers. Every owner shall be a member of the owners' forum and so shall be the worker of the workers' forum. These two forums shall perform duties to serve the national interest on the basis of mutual cooperation and adjustment. In case of any lapse in the performance of such duties, the State would give necessary directions and even impose its control. The apostles of fascism claim that by this arrangement by the corporate State, it would be possible to discard Marxian class struggle and to ensure class conciliation which, they think, liberalism has failed to achieve. Thus, the fascists claim that the corporate State they propagate is a superior and very successful political system compared to the liberal democratic system and the Marxian socialist system.

Fascism admittedly is an ideology based not on reason but blind faith. This blind faith undoubtedly is fostered by the myth which produces some utopian ideas. Indeed, the fascist conception of nation and the State is clearly a myth unsupported by facts of life. Further, when on the basis of this myth fascism views the State as the only watchdog of nation, it gives birth to an unwarranted thesis. It may be added that in the name of nation, fascism justifies an omnipotent State that negates freedom of the individual. Modern theorists take it as totally unacceptable. Moreover, fascism advises the State to take to the policy of violence and force, and regards it as the basis of the authority of the State. On the other hand, it glorifies war and imperialism which is opposed to world peace, the universally accepted ideal in the modern world. Last, fascism rejects democracy but fails to suggest an alternative viable system. Indeed, the corporate State it propagates is no match for a democratic State. No wonder the modern world marked by the triumph of democracy views fascism as a dangerous ideology.

Notes

GANDHISM

A 20th-century ideology, Gandhism originated in India under the sole initiative of M. K. Gandhi, one of India's seminal minds. As pointed out earlier, though having all the potentials of being the ruling principle of a political system, Gandhism has never been used as the ideological foundation of a political system. The fault, however, does not lie with this ideology but with those Indian political leaders who in the post-Independence period undertook the responsibility of building a sovereign State for India, disavowing the legacy of Gandhism. Yet the fact remains that Gandhi himself during India's struggle for freedom successfully experimented some of the elements of the ideology he invented, and further this ideology served as an inspiring force behind the civil rights movement in the USA and Africa and also the unilateral nuclear disarmament movement launched by Bertrand Russell in Britain. No wonder Gandhism has earned worldwide acclaim and recognition. Perhaps it would not be an overstatement to say that Gandhism is India's best gift to the world. In many ways, Gandhism has unique features that differentiate it from all other ideologies including even liberalism.

Gandhi made no secret of the fact that his ideology was essentially based on religion and morality. True, in this matter he was influenced by some Western thinkers. Yet his ideology was original, for he so adroitly intermixed the elements derived from Western sources with traditional Indian thinking that even today it is regarded as an ideology with no parallel in the world. In 1907, while behind the bars in South Africa, Gandhi for the first time became familiar with the ideas of Thoreau and immediately fell under their influence. Similarly, he drew inspiration from the ideas of Ruskin and Tolstoy. He accommodated these rather anarchist ideas with the teachings of India's Bhagavad Gita, Upanishads, Ramayana and Mahabharata, the Yoga Sutras of Patanjali and of the Buddhist and Jain religion, and constructed his own ideology. Thus, Gandhism represents a bridge between the East and the West.

Obviously, the keynote of the philosophy underlying Gandhism was religion. He viewed religion as an integral part of man's life. He also regarded himself as a person whose life was conditioned by religion and theism. Further, he considered politics with which he had life-long association as intertwined with religion. According to him, as religion attributes moral qualities to all human action, politics, essentially a human activity, cannot delink itself from religion. In one of his writings published in *Young India*, he expressed his firm belief that 'politics bereft of religion are a death-trap' for man. However, his idea of religion and God is somewhat different from what is in vogue. In his opinion, God represents truth and non-violence. In his autobiography, he declares that there is no other God than truth, and the only means to get at truth is *Ahimsa* (non-violence).

Notes

Naturally, to him to pursue truth and non-violence is religion. Truth that represents God, he continues further, comes out of man's 'inner voice', that is, his awakened moral conscience which purifies soul and directs man to stand for what is just and to fight against what is unjust. However, to fully develop this moral conscience, man needs to imbibe humility and when this humility reaches its final fulfilment it results in Gandhian non-violence.

While explaining the nature of non-violence, Gandhi begins with the premise that a perfect vision of truth is possible only on the basis of a complete realization of the ideal of non-violence. That is, non-violence is the finest human virtue that helps man get to God. The ideal and principles for developing this virtue, according to Gandhi, are as follows: First, to follow non-violence in the negative sense, what is required in thought, words and action is to do harm to none, not to physically strike anyone and desist from taking away the life of others. Second, in the positive sense, non-violence means to abjure hatred and evil motive and to love all including the enemy, the adversary and even the harmful one. That is, to follow non-violence, one has to bear with all sufferings caused by any evildoing and yet to love the evil-doer without any hatred and hostility towards him. But to love the wrongdoer is not to submit to his wrong. From this follows the third principle that non-violence is no cowardice or weakness. It is only forgiveness. However, only the brave and the fearless can be forgiving and not the coward and the weak. Fourth, non-violence is based on the principle of non-possession or what Gandhi calls *aparigraha.* To Gandhi, this non-possession is extremely important, for he believes that possession with no bar is opposed to love.

Besides, it is this possession that encourages the tendency to exploit. Therefore, he who claims no title to anything can follow the principle of non-violence. Fifth, to follow non-violence, one must be truthful without fail. Telling unpleasant truth is also permissible provided it is said gently and tenderly. However, when truth is spoken with a violent purpose, that is, when it is intended to do harm to any opponent, it must be avoided. Sixth, an essential condition for truly following non-violence is celibacy (Gandhi calls it *brahmacharya,* which he defines as control of the sense in thought, word and deed). Gandhi admits that to observe celibacy is a very difficult task for an ordinary mortal. Yet he insists that taking it as an ideal, one has to give the best of his efforts to realize it. Last, according to Gandhi, 'the needs of the body must be supplied by the body'.

Hence, in his opinion, physical labour is one of the important moral principles in life. It is with this physical labour that one learns to render service to others, which generates pure love in man that signifies the primary step to non-violence. This philosophy enunciated by Gandhi, though apparently looks like based on religion, is actually a moral philosophy. The goal of this philosophy is to rouse the spiritual strength of self whereby, by continuous exercise of truth

Notes

and non-violence, every man may arm himself with moral power and thus become truly a man.

One of the important elements of Gandhism is the idea of *swaraj* (self-rule). True, much before Gandhi, Bal Gangadhar Tilak introduced the idea of swaraj. Again, Dadabhai Naoroji as president of the Congress session held in 1906 also spoke of swaraj. However, they meant swaraj as the political independence of dependent India. Gandhi of course struggled for swaraj of the country. But he felt that if the individual is not ready for it, if he fails to free his mind and soul, swaraj of the nation will be fruitless. It was his firm decision that before achieving swaraj for the country, the individual himself has to attain swaraj, as in his opinion, 'the individual is the one supreme consideration'. Naturally, Gandhi began his idea of swaraj with the swaraj of the individual which mainly means freedom of the individual.

According to Gandhi, the ways an individual may have freedom for himself are as follows: First, man should be completely free to choose his task, that is, to decide how he will lead his life. Hence, the moral responsibility for all his work and decision is only his. For this, he cannot attribute responsibility to others or, for that matter, to his social environment. Second, he has the right to strive for self-development and, accordingly, he has every right to have freedom to apply his moral power for achieving self-development. Third, freed from all fear and coercion, that is, from obligation to others, he has the freedom to work voluntarily, for any work done under compulsion cannot be said to be moral. Fourth, man cannot enjoy his freedom in isolation. It is only by accepting the importance of social environment, by considering himself as a part of this environment and also by imbibing the social values reared by it that he may enjoy his freedom. Fifth, freedom of the individual is essentially his inner freedom. Hence, he enjoys true swaraj of himself whenever fearlessness is born out of his exercise for self-development. It is this fearlessness that enables the free individual to fight against the state and the external force like imperialism and also to face death.

According to Gandhi, 'Swaraj of a people means the sum total of the swaraj of individuals.' Naturally, Gandhi believes that society and the State may attain swaraj only in the way in which the individual earns his swaraj. He argues that as in the individual, in the society freedom is the main condition for swaraj. This freedom of society according to him may not be had by the principle of the greatest good of the majority but by ensuring maximum welfare for all. That is, freedom of society is universal. He calls this universal freedom *sarvodaya.* In other words according to him true social freedom flourishes in a sarvodaya society. He further argues that majority rule of modern parliamentary democracy is unfitted to this society. On the other hand, the social freedom established by this sarvodaya society should not be unrestricted. Control is indeed necessary to see

Notes

to it that one enjoys his freedom without interfering with the enjoyment of freedom by others. To Gandhi, liberation from the British rule was no doubt an essential condition for attaining swaraj of his nation. But he was convinced that even in an independent country, aggression on freedom may come from other sources. Hence, in his view, political independence of India was just a step towards realizing swaraj. Indeed, to him swaraj meant liberation from all kinds of bondage. Further, if in a society, an individual for his freedom and dignity depends too much on the State, the ideal of swaraj eludes it.

Swaraj truly is established in a society where the individual without relying on the State is a guardian of his freedom and dignity. Again, according to Gandhi, for the fullest development of a sarvodaya society, universal freedom alone is not enough; what is also needed is a social condition where all get equal opportunities for self-development, that is, where equality prevails. To him, of all kinds of equality, economic equality is the most important, which he believes is possible through equal distribution of wealth. But he feels that in actual practice, it is difficult, if not impossible, to give effect to equal distribution. Hence, he opts for equitable distribution.

Another important premise of Gandhism is that the ideal of sarvodaya reflected through the attainment of universal freedom on the basis of non-violence may be effectively realized only when the individual is able to apply adequate method for fighting out any external force attacking his freedom and rights. Gandhi styles this method as satyagraha. To him, this is the best instrument at the hands of the individual to guard his freedom and also that of others. At the very beginning of explaining the nature of this satyagraha, Gandhi makes it clear that satyagraha is completely different from passive resistance propagated mostly by Aurobindo Ghose in India. According to Gandhi, satyagraha, unlike passive resistance, is positive, direct and active resistance. The four principal features of satyagraha identified by him are as follows: non-violence, impersonal purpose, fearlessness and creativity. Satyagraha is non-violent in that one who uses this instrument never disrespects or hates the wrongdoer; on the contrary, he loves him. Naturally, he does not oppose him; all his resistance is against the wrong committed by him. Thus, he does not apply force against him nor does he coerce him. His only purpose is to change the heart of the wrongdoer by his own conduct. Thus, he must always subject himself to self-suffering as by it, he may prove that he loves and respects the evil-doer and this way may win his heart. Second, when one who takes to satyagraha is engaged in resistance, the purpose of this resistance is completely impersonal with a large perspective, for his target of attack is never the evil-doer. On the contrary, his purpose is to secure the greatest welfare to all. Thus, it has a much larger perspective, and since it is not directed to any particular person or group it is really impersonal. But this calls for immense moral strength which requires an active participant in satyagraha to develop moral qualities, the most important among which is fearlessness. Indeed, it is Gandhi's firm conviction that it is impossible for a coward to earn moral virtues. He who is fearless and may even sacrifice his life for winning the heart of the opponent is alone worthy of satyagraha.

Hence, according to Gandhi, fearlessness is the third important feature of satyagraha. Fourth, satyagraha is by nature creative. Because by changing the heart of the wrongdoer, it transforms him into a new man, that is, creates a moral man. Again, by effecting a moral transformation of society it gives it a new character and contributes much towards establishing justice in society. It may be mentioned that Gandhi not just confined satyagraha within the realm of ideas but put it into practice with immense success again and again during India's freedom struggle.

As a political ideology, Gandhism of course includes an idea of the State. How Gandhi viewed the State may be best known from his noted work *Hind Swaraj* published in 1909. But before penning this book, Gandhi in 1893 read Tolstoy's *The Kingdom of God Is within You* and in 1904 read Ruskin's *Unto This Last.* He was much influenced by the anarchist idea reflected in these books. Naturally, his idea of the State as presented in *Hind Swaraj* comes very close to the anarchist thought. That Gandhi all along held to his anarchism was proved in 1939 when he commented that after re-reading his *Hind Swaraj,* he felt no need to revise its ideas.

Obviously, the anarchist Gandhi unfavourably viewed the State. His aversion to the State was for several reasons. First, a believer in swaraj, Gandhi valued much the freedom of the individual. But he felt that absolute authority of the State poses a danger to individual freedom. Second, an apostle of non-violence, Gandhi was opposed to violence and physical force. But according to him, physical force is the basis of the State which represents nothing but organized and centralized violence and force. Third, the State destroys individuality of man which indeed is the source of social progress. Fourth, every individual has a soul, but the State is just a machine devoid of soul. Last, power is inevitably concentrated in the State. But this kills the desire of the individual to attain his swaraj by his own worth. In the same way, he was much against the parliamentary democratic system of the West. Interestingly, he likened the British Parliament to an infertile woman, as he felt that it was impossible for it to take an independent and effective move.

On the other hand, he subjected the British parliamentary democratic system to severe criticism. He believed that in this system, the prime minister is only interested in the enjoyment and expansion of his power and also in the prioritization of party interest rather than public interest. On the other hand, he was convinced that in the entire British political system, there was only dominance of party interest.

Notes

Gandhi's aversion towards the State and the parliamentary democratic system is all due to the fact that he was much against centralization of power he noticed in the State and the parliamentary system, as he felt that this centralization would endanger the individual swaraj. Indeed, he made the strongest plea for decentralization of power. In the interest of this decentralization of power, he wanted to replace the vertical power structure by a horizontal power structure which would ensure decentralization.

But what would be the ideal system involving horizontal power structure and decentralization of power? Gandhi gave an answer to this question in his essay published in the *Harijan* paper on 28 July 1946. In this article, he introduced the idea of 'gram swaraj' which he underscored as the ideal system. Gandhi explained that in this system of gram swaraj, every village would be a republic or a 'panchayat' where all the villagers would participate in decision-making; that is, all power would vest in them. Every village would be self-sufficient, which would manage everything related to it and also protect itself from any external attack. It may take help from outside only when this help comes based on spontaneous cooperation and also voluntarily. The individual would remain at the centre of this system. In the interest of gram swaraj, he would always remain ready for self-sacrifice and also to lay down his life. Non-violence would be the governing principle of the gram swaraj. The relation between villages would be completely free from any domination and subordination. The villages together would form a circle where all would be equal and, as a result, every village would be equally powerful. The individual would remain at the centre of this circle of villages. As he has to make self-sacrifice for his village, he would sacrifice himself for this circle. He would have no impudence, but only humility. Gandhi believed that in this way by virtue of self-rule and cooperation the gram swaraj would be quite powerful. This however would not affect in any way the individual swaraj, for no one would apply any force on the individual who spontaneously would accept self-control.

Gandhism with its very many distinctive aspects is no doubt a unique ideology. But its applicability and practicability are surely open to question. Its attempt to base politics just on religion and morality is obsolete in the modern world, as it denies politics an autonomous status so widely accepted in our time. Again, it dismisses the State but, unlike Marxism, does not go deep into the question. It discards the State just on the ground that it is an embodiment of force. But that is not enough. After all, liberal thinkers beginning with T. H. Green have shown with convincing arguments that despite the fact that the State monopolizes the right to apply maximum force, it may serve the individual and secure his freedom. The main defect of Gandhism is that in no case it adduces sufficient logical arguments in support of the thesis it establishes. The reason behind this is that Gandhism relies more on faith than on reason, more on the so-called 'inner voice' (which Jinnah, the Muslim League leader of India, often used to ridicule) than on external conditions. This is why Gandhism has often been criticized as a utopian ideology.

Notes

Yet Gandhism has no doubt a few merits for which it has occupied a permanent place in world history. First, it is the only ideology that emphasizes that man needs to develop moral virtue in order to deserve his freedom. That is, his message is that a free citizen should essentially be a good man (a question Aristotle failed to resolve), which is surely valid for all kinds of political systems. Second, through its anti-State stand, it issues a warning that an extremely powerful State may sometimes turn into a police State, threatening the freedom of the individual—a warning which has been found to be true in the overdoings of even some democratic systems in the modern world. Third, dependence of Gandhism on non-violence may sound too moralistic to be followed in ordinary life. But it has a grain of truth in that it implies that violence, if carried to an extreme, may pose a threat to the survival of human civilization. It is, no doubt, being proved by the recent senseless terrorist activities across the world. Last, satyagraha, an integral part of Gandhism, may appear extremely difficult to cultivate. But throughout Gandhi's political career, hundreds of thousands of political workers of India joined the satyagraha movement under his leadership and, as already pointed out, in the latter-day world too it has not gone obsolete. This indeed has given Gandhism a kind of immortality.

15
CHAPTER

Government

Notes

INTRODUCTION

In popular view, a government represents a body comprising the political and bureaucratic executive which formulates policies, makes decisions and implements them. However, it is a wrong view. The term government has a much wider dimension. Actually, a government presupposes a holistic system that includes the legislature, the executive and the judiciary—the three branches that together constitute a government. These three organs work according to long-established rules. Thus, the legislature enacts laws, the executive implements such laws and the task of the judiciary is to take appropriate measures in case these laws are violated. In modern times, the orbit of work of these three organs has much expanded. However, they all follow the standing norm that one will not do the function of the other nor will it interfere with the functions of the latter. That is, they work more or less autonomously. But this autonomy does not mean isolation; that is, it is not that they attend to their respective responsibilities with no relation or connection among themselves.

Just the contrary was propagated by the French political thinker Montesquieu and English jurist Blackstone in the 18th century. They advocated what is known as the theory of separation of powers that recommends a strict separation of powers and functions between the three organs of government as they felt that this would safeguard freedom of the individual. But this theory has now been outdated as it has been a universal experience that in actual practice

Notes

it is impossible to maintain a rigid compartmentalization between the three branches of government. True, the US political system began its journey following Montesquieu and Blackstone. But over the years, it has been proved to be impracticable. Thus, it is found today that even in the US system, one department has to accept at least indirect assistance from the other. Hence, it is universally agreed in our times that none of the branches of government may act as an insulated island, that they are indeed organically related to each other.

THE LEGISLATURE

In every liberal democratic system, legislature plays a pivotal role, for it is the only institution that puts into practice popular sovereignty, which is the principal ideal of liberal democracy. However, the way it is formed and its structure and functions differ from country to country. Of course, the lower house of the legislature is everywhere directly elected by the people, though it is differently designated in different countries. The upper house of the legislature however is not everywhere, though in a federal system it is an essential requirement. The structure and functions of the upper house, however, differ from country to country. The upper house of the legislature is usually a permanent body, though in countries such as the USA and India, one-third of its members retire after a certain period and the vacant seats are filled by virtue of election. On the other hand, in Canada members of the upper house are all nominated. In Britain, a part of the members are nominated and the other part get membership by inheritance. In Ireland and India, a part of the members are nominated while the other part are elected. In the USA however all the members are elected. In almost all the countries, members of the upper house are indirectly elected. For instance, in India the members of the upper house of the central legislature are elected by the elected members of State Legislative Assemblies. The USA however is an exception in this respect. After the 17th Constitutional Amendment, all the members of the Senate, the upper house of the national legislature Congress, are directly elected by the people. In most of the federal systems such as the USA, the upper house of the national legislature is constituted by equal number of members elected from the constituent states. But in certain cases, as in India, the upper house of the national legislature is not constituted on the basis of equal representation.

Usually, the two houses of the legislature are not of equal power. For instance, the House of Lords, the upper house of the British Parliament is virtually powerless. The Indian Constitution apparently gives equal powers in the passing of bills to the Council of States, the upper house, and the House of the People, the lower house of the Indian Parliament. However, in actual

Notes

practice, the upper house enjoys lesser powers than the lower house, for in case of disagreement between the two houses in the matter relating to passing of any bill (except a money bill and a constitutional amendment bill), the Constitution provides for a joint session of the two houses to decide the fate of the bill. But because of the far superior numerical strength of the lower house, the will of the lower house always prevails. However, in case of disagreement on a constitutional amendment bill, there is no provision for joint meeting, which clearly establishes that on that score, the upper house shares the same power with the lower house. But in case of introducing and passing of a money bill, the upper house has no power except delaying the passing of the money bill for a fortnight. Contrary is the case in the USA. Here, the Senate, the upper house of the Congress, has greater power than the House of Representatives, the lower house. In matters relating to foreign affairs, the Senate has the supreme authority. Further, the Senate dominates in central legislation and even in financial matters. In fact, the American Senate is recognized as the most powerful upper house in the world.

The functions of the legislature are multiple. In parliamentary democracy like Britain and India, the Council of Ministers are born out of the lower house of the legislature; that is, the party commanding majority in the lower house forms the government. Further, the stability of the government is dependent on the lower house of the legislature, for if it loses the majority support of the lower house, it must resign. Thus, in a parliamentary democracy, the primary function of the legislature is to form the government and to keep it going. Bagehot, an English writer, in his celebrated work *The English Constitution* has called it the elective function of the legislature. In the presidential system like the USA however the legislature has no role in forming the government. The president, the chief executive, is straightaway elected and he appoints his ministers as per his own choice. Yet the legislature has some functions vis-à-vis the government. For instance, in the US system, the appointment of all high officials by the president and all international agreements and treaties signed by him are subject to approval by the Senate. In Switzerland, the national legislature elects members of the Federal Council, the national executive and also the federal judges. In India, the president, the formal head of government, is elected by the elected members of both the houses of the Parliament and also by the elected members of the State Legislative Assemblies. The vice-president is elected by members of both the houses of Parliament.

Both in the presidential and parliamentary forms of government, the legislature is constituted by people's representatives. Obviously, people's will, expectations and opinions are all reflected through it. In other words, the legislature truly expresses the mind of the people. No wonder Bagehot calls it the expressive function of the legislature. Again, the legislature is a forum for debate and

Notes

discussion. All this centres round the government's policy and programme, all social and economic problems of the country as well as matters related to public interest. This is what renders political teaching to the people and rouses their political consciousness. According to Bagehot, this actually is the teaching function of the legislature. Further, by way of its deliberations and daily routine, the legislature constantly communicates to the people data and information on government policies, administration, foreign policy, economic policy and so on, which greatly benefits the citizens. Bagehot calls this the informing function of the legislature.

According to Bagehot, the last but not the least important function of the legislature is legislation. To run the State appropriately, various laws are necessary. Further, to cope with the needs of the changing time, it becomes necessary to change a law or repeal it. All this is the exclusive responsibility of the legislature. Throughout the entire process of passing a bill, the legislature minutely examines every aspect of the bill. In modern times, there are various legislative committees to help the legislature in this function. Since a legislative committee is a small body, it is better able to examine the details of the bill. As a result, the task of legislation becomes easier for the legislature. In the US system, these legislative committees are extremely powerful.

They can completely change the text of the bill concerned except changing its title. Comparatively, the British and Indian committees are less powerful. They cannot alter the principles and purpose of the proposed bill.

Besides the functions identified by Bagehot, the legislature has other functions as well. For instance, first in a democracy the government can make no expenses, impose no taxes and receive no debt without due approval of the legislature. Again, the government is under compulsion to place its annual budget in the legislature and get its approval. Thus, the legislature has complete control over the income and expenditure of the government. Second, in almost all the countries, the legislature enjoys constituent power, that is, the power of making and amending the constitution. While exercising this power, the British Parliament is subject to no condition. It can make any new constitutional law or amend it by following the procedure of ordinary law making. On the other hand, in the US system constitutional amendment is possible only by the support of two-thirds members of the national legislature and by the approval of threefourths of State legislatures. In India also, some parts of the Constitution may be amended only by two-thirds majority of the members of Parliament, together with the endorsement of at least half of the State legislatures. Third, the legislature has some judicial powers as well. For instance, in Britain the Law Lords of the upper house constitute a body that works as the highest court of appeal in Britain. Recently, however, this body goes by the name of Supreme

Notes

Court. Yet the members of this body are all drawn only from the House of Lords, the upper house. In the USA, a proposal for removing the president on grounds of proven incapacity or misbehaviour, that is, the proposal for impeachment, may be brought in the lower house and the upper house judges the validity of the charges against the president. Whenever the upper house sits to enquire into these charges, it is chaired by the Chief Justice of the Supreme Court. In India also, the president may be impeached only on the ground of violation of the Constitution by Parliament. Fourth, the legislature has some investigative functions as well. Thus, whenever the nation is confronted with a disturbing problem or when there is a serious charge against any high government functionary or a government organization, the legislature with some of its members forms a committee that investigates the matter and submits its report. What action has been taken by the government on this report is placed before the legislature which is discussed in detail in the latter.

Thus, the legislature has very many functions. However, its major function is to legislate. Unfortunately, in recent times in democratic systems, particularly in a parliamentary democracy, the legislature has virtually lost its exclusive power of making laws. That is, there has been a steady decline of the powers of legislature. This is due to various reasons. First, in a parliamentary democracy, the draft of every bill is prepared by the departmental minister with the aid of the bureaucrats working under him. No matter whatever debate and discussion on this bill be held in the legislature, it is invariably passed by it by virtue of the support of the majority of members belonging to the ruling party. That is, the legislature makes a law as desired by the government. Thus, a law is made by the government which only gets a formal approval of the legislature. In a parliamentary democracy, this is called cabinet dictatorship which to a large extent usurps the power of parliament.

In a presidential form of democracy however the legislature monopolizes the power of law making in which the executive has little scope to interfere. Yet as is found in the presidential system of the USA, the Congress, the national legislature, usually does not make a law not desired by the president. This is because the president utilizes the opportunity of influencing the legislature by consulting in advance its members (which is known as lobbying) and also by distributing various rewards among them (technically known as the spoils system). This is how the executive there intrudes frequently into the legislative work. Besides in the US system, a bill duly passed by the Congress may become a law after it is approved by the president. This power of approval is not just a formal power but a real power of the president, for if the president exercises his veto power, that is, disapproves the bill concerned, it has to be passed again by both the houses of Congress by two-thirds majority, which usually is not an easy task because of uneven party strength. Sometimes, just by holding the threat of exercising his veto, the president brings the Congress under his control. As K. C. Wheare rightly points out, in the US system, this presidential veto is not a 'dead letter' as it is frequently used.

Further, as there has been a plethoric rise in the needs and problems of modern life, the legislature has to make plenty of laws within a fixed time. But since it is always a very large body, it may not be possible for it to fully complete its task of law making within the limited time. This is why in modern democracy most of the legislatures, while legislating, attend to passing the basic framework of law embodying its purposes and principles, and leave the remainder to be done by the relevant government administration which gives the fullest shape to it. In constitutional parlance, this is known as delegated legislation. This delegated legislation, though coming to the aid of legislature, obviously abridges the role of legislature.

Again, there was a time in England when membership of parliament was not a paid job and when political stalwarts and important public figures used to be its members. Today in England, because of the developed party system, party members, even though they do not have first-rate political worth, become members of parliament. This also accounts for decline of legislature. It may not be out of context to mention that in this respect the conditions in India are much worse. At the beginning of post-Independence India, historic freedom fighters, eminent jurists and social activists were members of the Indian Parliament. But with their mortal departure and with gradual erosion of values, the Indian Parliament today has turned into a club house of so-called commoners, professionals and even persons with criminal records who, least concerned about the power and dignity of Parliament, indulge in the politics of wrangling and noise, and even stall the proceedings of the house in the name of protest. Thus, the fast-changing social composition of members of legislature is also a reason for its decline.

That however does not minimize the importance of legislature as an organ of government. After all, it is not the only job of legislature to make laws and dislodge the ruling executive in a parliamentary democracy. It works as a symbol of popular sovereignty which constitutes the very essence of democracy. Further, democracy requires a formal forum where public opinion is freely reflected. The legislature represents this forum. Again, through the debate and discussion held in the legislature, every information on national and international politics is communicated to the people, which helps in forming public opinion. Last, in order that people may correctly evaluate the performance of the executive, they need to be aware of what is said by members of the executive and members of the ruling party and also what is said by opposition members in the legislature. This also proves the crucial role of the legislature. No wonder

Notes

Bernard Crick underscores the supreme importance of this function of the legislature.

THE EXECUTIVE

The executive is no less an important organ of the government as it is in sole charge of governance. A political system is mostly known by how its executive is structured and how it functions. The executive in every system has two parts. One is known as political executive and the other as non-political executive. The chief executive, together with other members of the executive body, represents the political part. In a parliamentary system, the king or queen as in Britain or the president and the vice-president as in India and the council of ministers with the prime minister at its top are known as political executives. In a presidential system like the USA, the president along with the ministers (designated as secretaries of the State) working under him represents the political executive. In a parliamentary system, except the hereditary constitutional functionaries like the king or the queen, all other members of the executive are elected functionaries. In the presidential system like the USA, only the president, the chief executive, is an elected functionary. The ministers are his appointees and hold office during his pleasure. In a parliamentary system like the UK and India, the council of ministers are collectively responsible to the lower house of the legislature. But in a presidential system, the president together with his subordinate ministers works independently of the legislature. Since the president in a presidential system and the Council of Ministers (and also the president and vice-president in India) all work for a certain term, they are treated as the non-permanent part of the executive. The non-political executive comprises of the civil servants, bureaucrats and all employees working in civil capacity. Since they are not politically recruited, that is, not elected but appointed by the appropriate authority, they represent the non-political part of the executive. Again, as they hold office for a long period without break, they are regarded as the permanent part of the executive.

The structure of the executive varies depending on the nature of the political system. For instance, in a parliamentary system, the executive has at its top a nominal head like the hereditary queen or king in Britain or an elected president as in India. The entire administration runs in her or his name. Yet this formal head has very little real power. All real power is exercised by an elected Council of Ministers, headed by the prime minister. It is this prime minister who is considered as the chief executive. On the other hand, in a presidential form such as the US system, the executive is headed by an elected president who is not only the head of the State but also the supreme arbiter of administration. Naturally, he alone is regarded as the chief executive. There is of course a group of ministers to

Notes

assist him in his work. But they are not elected to their office. The president appoints them as per his choice and they work subordinate to the president.

Obviously in the presidential system, a single executive is in charge of governance. On the contrary, since in a parliamentary system, the Council of Ministers together with the prime minster jointly runs the administration, it is rightly regarded as an example of collective executive. There may be a plural executive as well. For instance, in Switzerland, the Federal Council, which is the national executive, is constituted by seven members with equal power. One among these seven members is appointed by rotation the President of the Council for one year.

However, the president or any member can in no way influence the other members. On the other hand, the French political system represents a combination of single executive and collective executive. A Council of Ministers led by the prime minister runs the administration there. They are responsible to the lower house of the national legislature; that is, if they do not have the majority support of the lower house they must resign, though they are not members of the legislature. Side by side with this, there is an elected president. In normal circumstances, he does not interfere with the administration run by the Council of Ministers. But he presides over the meeting of the Council of Ministers and in that capacity may very well influence the decision of the Council of Ministers. Besides, in national emergency, he may take over the entire power of the Council of Ministers.

A modern democratic State is not just a police State, it is more a welfare State. In modern times, the needs and demands of people for welfare have been fast rising. As a result, compared to the past, the executive of a modern democratic State has to attend to much greater responsibilities which have far widened the area of its functions. The most important of these functions is, no doubt, to govern efficiently. This involves maintaining law and order as well as drawing up newer welfare schemes. Naturally, the executive has to take to various policies in order to look after public health, education, food and so on. At the same time, it has to adopt appropriate measures to implement law and guard against its violation. To provide such necessary services, it appoints a large army of officers and workers as well as police personnel and keeps them under control. Second, all matters relating to war and defence come under the jurisdiction of the executive. Third, in a parliamentary democracy it is the function of the executive to prepare the draft of a bill and place it before the legislature. Further, the executive prepares the budget, proposes earning of revenue by imposing taxes and from other sources collects revenue and incurs expenditure. Fourth, whenever the legislature is not in session, it may issue ordinances which are treated as good as law. Fifth, by taking advantage of delegated legislation, it takes an important role in the making of law. In a presidential democracy, the functions of the executive

Notes

are not so extensive. However, unlike in a parliamentary system, the presidential executive functions independently of the legislature, and as noted earlier a president with strong personality and dexterity can get the legislature to make a law suited to his convenience. The executive also has some judicial function in that it can remit or pardon the punishment given by the judiciary.

With the advancement of civilization, as human life invites newer necessities, it begets continuously new problems. To meet these needs and combat these problems, the modern executive has been undertaking greater responsibilities. Thus, the modern executive has to draw up policies and programmes on matters such as scientific research, development of nuclear power, conservation of forest, wildlife and natural environment, fighting with the problem of environment, nationalization or disinvestment of industries and expansion of information technology. Obviously, this has led to the widening of the executive functions.

Chief Executive

Leadership in all these functions is given by the chief executive. Therefore, an account of the functions of the executive cannot be complete without an evaluation of the role of the chief executive. In a presidential system like the USA, the president is the chief executive. On the other hand, in a parliamentary system like Britain and India, the chief executive is the prime minister. The US Constitution vests all executive power on the president. Accordingly, the president as the chief executive alone runs the administration. He is the architect of all policies, decisions and steps taken by the national government. In every matter in this regard, his is the last word. True, under him works a body of ministers to assist him. But the president does not have to share power with them. They virtually are like high officials working under him to carry out his decisions and implement policies formulated by him. On the other hand, in a parliamentary system, though the prime minister is recognized as the chief executive, the Council of Ministers collectively exercises executive power, and in it the prime minister is treated as *primus inter pares*, that is, first among equals. Naturally, he does not singly exercise executive power; that is, he is not the supreme authority in governance.

Thus, apparently it may mean that in the context of the exercise of executive power, the president as the chief executive of a presidential system is far more powerful than the prime minister as the chief executive of a parliamentary system. However, in actual practice and in the modern context, there is not really much difference between these two chief executives. In fact, the very nature of executive power is to concentrate. The US Constitution has constitutionally facilitated this concentration of power at the hands of the president. On the contrary, the constitution of a parliamentary democracy like Britain and India formally diffuses executive power in the Council of Ministers instead of vesting it in the prime minister alone. However, in actual practice, it is often witnessed that if the prime minister is tactful and discreet and further is gifted with a strong personality, he may hold the entire Council of Ministers under his sway. Thus, in terms of power, the prime minister may almost be equal to the president.

In modern times, the prime minister in a parliamentary system has been as much powerful as the president of a presidential system for several reasons.

First, his personal worth, intelligence and experience give him such a position of dignity in the Council of Ministers that other ministers take him as their indubitable leader, deserving their respect, and spontaneously endorse his decision and opinion. Second, by demonstrating his personal qualities and skill, and in certain cases by virtue of dramatization of reality, a prime minister always tries to achieve charismatic leadership. The more he attains this charisma and is able to establish a strong base of leadership among the people, the more he becomes powerful and, in view of his halo of power, the ministers do not dare opposing his decision. Third, in the US system, the president is able to successfully address all complex problems of administration because, since 1939, to assist him in his work there has been functioning an extra-constitutional body known as Executive Office. Recently, as a part of this body, president's personal office, known as White House Office, is at work comprising president's personal advisers chosen by him. With the aid of these personal advisers, the president alone takes decisions and for this he does not at all depend on his ministers. It may be noted that in a modern parliamentary system too, a similar kind of advisory group is at work. For instance, in Britain and India, the recent practice is to have a Prime Minister's Office, a body which has neither constitutional nor statutory support and is composed of specialists and experts appointed directly by the prime minister. This office provides assistance and advice to the prime minister in making policies and taking decisions. The prime minster depends more on this office than on the ministers. In fact, with the help of this body of experts, the prime minister has been so powerful that the parliamentary government sometimes verges almost on a prime ministerial government as exemplified by Margaret Thatcher in Britain and Indira Gandhi in India.

Fourth, in a presidential democracy, the president has no scope to provide legislative leadership, though by applying his veto, he may force the legislature to pass a bill again by the support of a special majority. On the contrary, as noted earlier, in a parliamentary system, in matters of law making, the executive plays a major role. Obviously, as the chief executive and as leader of the legislature, the prime minister provides legislative leadership. On that score, the prime minister of the parliamentary system is more powerful than the president of the presidential system.

Notes

It may be added that in a democracy, the chief executive is not only the leader of his party and government but also the supreme leader of the people. All attention is focused on what he says and how he runs the government, and it is on this consideration that his popularity is judged. As he is aware of it, he continuously tries to enhance his popularity so that he may firmly establish himself as an accepted leader of the people. The more he is able to do so, the greater is his authority. No wonder he always tries to brighten his image and accordingly tries to establish himself as a leader of the people. With this end in view, he tries to develop intimate and direct communication with people with the help of electronic media. In fact, in modern times it is this electronic media that is one of the factors in making the chief executive extremely powerful.

The part of the executive that implements the policies and decisions taken at the level of the political executive and thus keeps the administration going is known as the non-political executive. It is called non-political because its members do not occupy their office by way of any political competition but are recruited by an appropriate authority on the basis of their merit and are appointed by the government for a fairly long period. These members are known as bureaucrats or civil servants. The political executive comprises mainly amateurs and accordingly it depends, to a large extent, on the knowledge and experience of bureaucrats. This is why in every political system, particularly in a parliamentary democracy, bureaucracy is extremely powerful. Naturally, bureaucracy merits a separate discussion.

BUREAUCRACY

In the US presidential system, bureaucrats are all political appointees chosen by the president alone. Their only task is to carry out the orders of the president. Obviously, they do not have any scope to participate in the policymaking and decision-making of the president. Naturally, they do not have any independent power. Hence, bureaucracy poses no problem in the US system. On the other hand, in a parliamentary system such as Britain and India, bureaucrats are not political appointees. They are recruited by an independent agency on the basis of merit as well as their success in a competitive examination, and after appointment, they undergo a thorough training in administration. In France however this training is given prior to appointment. In any case, however, when they occupy office, they are already quite knowledgeable and by virtue of the fact that they serve for a long time, they are also very experienced in matters of administration. As a result, ministers representing the political executive very much depend on the bureaucrats serving under them for making of government policies and decisions. This naturally makes the bureaucrats very powerful and sometimes they become so powerful that they not only assist the ministers but also very much influence them. But, unlike ministers, they do not have any accountability to the legislature. As power without accountability may generate despotic tendencies, long ago the British writer Lord Hewart, watching the overpowerful bureaucracy in his country, described bureaucracy as 'New Despotism'. Thus, in a parliamentary democracy, bureaucracy may pose a threat to the very principle of democracy.

The German writer Max Weber for the first time developed a comprehensive theory of bureaucracy. He however not just viewed bureaucracy in the context of government but put it on the wider canvas of society, arguing that bureaucracy is an essential aspect of any social organization of modern industrial society. Yet Max Weber's theoretical stand is, of course, relevant to the study of politics. Weber identified certain characteristics of bureaucracy which are as follows: First, bureaucracy has a fixed jurisdiction determined by specific laws and regulations. Thus, a bureaucrat works on the basis of clearly defined powers and, subject to laws and regulations, he differentiates his official duties from duties in his private life. Second, he is subject to a hierarchy where the lower office is under the control and supervision of the higher office. Third, the bureaucratic administration is guided by written documents, that is, what is called service rules and is carried on according to definitive procedures that require specialized training. Fourth, recruitment of bureaucrats is made not on the basis of ascription but on the basis of personal achievement to be judged by means of examination meant for the purpose or academic attainment or by both. Fifth, the bureaucrat must be mentally prepared not to claim any right of ownership of the post he holds nor of the resources accompanying it. Last, the bureaucratic job is career-oriented with a fixed salary and with opportunities of promotion determined by seniority or efficiency.

Weber further argues that in view of these characteristics, bureaucracy functions as the most orderly, rational and efficient wing of administration. Weber no doubt has a point, for bureaucrats while working strictly follow a procedure defined by rules and regulations. They are also thoroughly impersonal and hence neutral in their dealings with their clientele. That is why bureaucracy represents a rational, orderly and objective set-up. Again, bureaucrats, in all democratic governments, enjoy security of tenure (in India, it is constitutionally guaranteed), pensions and gradual increment of salary, and they get promotion according to standing principles. All this encourages them to fully devote to their job. This is what ensures their efficiency and infuses into them a kind of professionalism. But this is only an ideal type. What Weber ignores is that in actual practice, the power enjoyed by bureaucracy tends to make it overpowerful in that in a parliamentary system, it may begin to think itself more vital than ministers in the making of policies and decisions.

As R. K. Merton points out, bureaucracy is liable to dysfunctions. According to him, the root of this dysfunction is in the very characteristics and operation

Notes

of bureaucracy. For instance, strict adherence to rules by bureaucrats brings about too much rigidity in their attitude and activities, and thus a prisoner of formalism, bureaucrats tend to lose their creativity and turn into mechanized robots, indulging in red tape that causes undesirable complexity and procrastination affecting services to be given to the clientele. Further, impersonalism of the bureaucrats may seriously affect human relations expected of them in their dealings with the clientele.

The only way out of this impasse is to evolve a responsive and a responsible bureaucracy. If bureaucrats accept that they have to remain constantly responsive to the ever-changing needs and demands of the people they serve and if they further accept that they, under no circumstances, may abjure their accountability to the ministers as well as to the people at large, they can very well be responsive and responsible. However, it is hard to expect that bureaucrats on their own will develop this mentality since there is no built-in mechanism in bureaucracy to that effect. What indeed is required is to charge them with democratic values. But only when the political executive itself imbibes these values, it may claim the right to inculcate democratic values among the bureaucrats. Thus, bureaucracy may truly be committed to democratic values only when the political executive goes by democratic culture.

THE JUDICIARY

In a democratic system, judiciary is a vital organ of government as it acts as a vigilant sentinel of a democratic as well as of a federal State. Its basic task is to assist the legislature in that it protects the laws made by it and gives appropriate punishment in case of violation of any of them. Besides, it is the fundamental duty of a democratic State to secure justice to everyone. It is the judiciary that attends to this duty by protecting individual interests and settling disputes between individuals.

Again, in a federal State the judiciary settles disputes between the Centre and the state or between different states. Further, in a federal State, there must be some neutral and judicious body to interpret the constitution and to act as its guardian. It is the judiciary that discharges this extremely important responsibility in a federal State.

The judicial system differs depending on whether it is a unitary State or a federal State. Thus, in Britain, a unitary State, there is a single judicial system. Here, at the lowest level there are two sets of courts—civil and criminal. Above them, there are two separate appeal courts. The final authority and the highest court to hear appeals from these appeal courts is the Supreme Court composed

Notes

of nine Law Lords of the House of Lords which is led by Lord Chancellor who is also a member of the cabinet. On the other hand, in a federal State like the USA, the judicial system is dual. That is, along with a judicial system at the national level, there is a separate judicial system in the constituent states. At the national level, the highest court is the Supreme Court, below which there are nine appeal courts and there are many district courts at the lowest level. Similarly, at the state level, the highest court is the Supreme Court, below which there are various courts to deal with civil and criminal cases. Generally, an appeal against the judgment of the State Supreme Court cannot be made to the federal Supreme Court barring those cases related with federal constitutional questions. In India, it may be noted, there is a single and integrated judicial system with the Supreme Court at its top.

The process of recruitment of judges differs from country to country. For instance, in France and Germany youths of a certain age with a law degree are recruited through a competitive examination and thereafter they are appointed judges of the lower courts. In course of time, by virtue of promotion, they become judges of the higher courts. In Britain, all judges are recruited from practising lawyers except the judges of the lowest courts. In the USA too, judges are recruited from among lawyers. In India, a part of the judges of the lowest court are recruited by means of a competitive examination and the other part from the lawyers. Through promotion, they may go to the higher levels and may be a high court judge or even a Supreme Court judge. A part of the judges of the high courts and the Supreme Court is directly recruited from lawyers on condition laid down by the Indian Constitution. However, their recruitment is subject to constitutional rules amended by a Supreme Court judgement. In the USA, the Supreme Court judges may work for an unlimited period, while in India they work up to a certain age fixed by the Constitution.

In every modern democratic system, the judiciary plays a very crucial role. No wonder in every democracy, its functions are on the rise. An analysis of these functions reveals its importance. These functions are mainly as follows: First, to secure justice to everyone belonging to a State is its chief and indeed the oldest function. For this purpose, it settles all disputes between an individual and the other, between an individual and any agency or organization and between the individual and the State. This settlement is made under laws made by the State. It is mandatory for all to obey this judgment. It is the responsibility of administration to give effect to this judgement.

Second, in recent times, in countries such as the USA, Britain and India, the judiciary renders not only legal justice but social justice as well. In order to make this effort fully effective, in recent times, cases known as public interest litigation case are allowed by the judiciary. In ordinary legal suits, one who is harmed may

Notes

alone move the court, following the specific procedure laid down by the court. But as regards public interest litigation, a responsible citizen who himself is not affected may file a suit praying justice for any other affected person. Further, the usual procedure and legal formalities are not at all necessary. In a country like India, where many, particularly the poor, are denied social justice, thousands of public interest litigation lawsuits are filed every year.

Third, protection of rights of citizens is also an important function of the judiciary. In countries such as the USA and India, the Constitution has guaranteed certain fundamental rights to the citizens and has also given the judiciary responsibility for protecting these rights. Accordingly, in case of violation of any of the fundamental rights, the higher judiciary is empowered to issue writs and orders as remedial measures. Since the British Constitution is unwritten, there is no constitutional system to identify the rights of the individual. However, since the British Constitution is governed by the rule of law, the judiciary there identifies these rights in the context of the rule of law and, of course, protects them.

Fourth, in all democratic countries, the legislature makes laws, both ordinary and constitutional, but is not empowered to interpret them. It is the judiciary which alone may interpret them. While set to the task of interpretation, it may make almost a new law and virtually amend the constitution. In fact, the US and Indian Constitutions have been so widely changed by the Supreme Court by some of its historic judgments that both these Constitutions are also regarded as judge-made law. Again, the judgment given by the highest judiciary is often used as a precedent in subsequent cases and that virtually gives the judgement of the judiciary the status of law. It may be noted that Article 141 of the Indian Constitution clearly gives status of law to the judgment of the Supreme Court and declares that it shall be binding on all courts of India.

Fifth, the judiciary has some advisory function as well. In India, Britain and Canada, for instance, the executive may seek advice of the judiciary on some important legal and constitutional questions. Even on a sensitive social or political problem, the executive may refer the matter to the judiciary. In India, this advisory function of the Supreme Court has been much used. Sixth, the judiciary frames rules for its internal administration. Further, the higher court supervises the power and function of the subordinate courts. Seventh, in a federal system, the federal court plays an important role. It establishes federal justice by settling disputes between different constituent states and also disputes between the federal government and a state government or several state governments. Last, in a federal system, the judiciary plays a vital role in keeping this system going. For instance, the constitution in a federal State divides powers between the Centre and the states and clearly determines relations between the two. Thus, the constitution represents the heart and soul of the federal system. The highest judiciary protects the constitution and interprets it. Further, if any law is enacted both at the level of the Centre and the states, the highest judiciary has the power to declare it void. This power is known as the power of judicial review which is frequently used by the US and Indian Supreme Courts. However, in this regard, the power of judicial review of the US Supreme Court is far greater than that of the Indian Supreme Court.

The judiciary has some other functions as well. For instance, in India, the higher judiciary settles disputes relating to elections. In the USA, when a proposal for impeachment of the president is passed by the House of Representatives and thereafter the Senate sits in judgement on it, the Chief Justice of the US Supreme Court presides over this session of the Senate. In India, if the president of India wants to remove the chairman or any other member of Public Service Commissions on grounds of proved misbehaviour or incapacity, he has to refer the matter to the Supreme Court which makes an enquiry into the charge and submits its report to the President. The management of the property of a deceased dying intestate, appointment of a guardian for an orphan and conservation of a disputed property are also the functions of the judiciary.

Independence of the Judiciary

The above-noted functions reveal that the judiciary is not just an agency to settle disputes. It is more an organization that establishes justice in the society and politics, protects rights of citizens, interprets all kinds of law and in a federal system acts as a guardian of the constitution. Thus, judiciary has immense contribution to the smooth working of the democratic process. But in order that judiciary may play this vital role, it must have independence. Thus, independence of the judiciary is an essential condition for its active and dynamic role. The ways to ensure this independence are the following.

In the first place, independence of the judiciary depends much on the procedure for their appointment. In all democratic countries, the executive appoints the judges. However, in almost all democratic countries except the USA, the judges are appointed strictly on the basis of merit and worth. In this respect, the Indian system presents a bright example. In India, a substantial section of judges of the lower courts are appointed by their merit and also success in a competitive examination held by an independent agency for their recruitment. The rest are nominated from among the working lawyers. However, this nomination is made on the basis of their worth and efficiency. In case of appointment of Supreme Court and High Court judges, the President, as formal head of government, appoints them subject to concurrence of the Chief Justice of India together with

Notes

four senior most judges of the Supreme Court. But in the USA, this appointment is made mostly on political considerations, which is inimical to the independence of the judiciary there.

Second, if judges work for a long time they attain greater experience, and by properly utilizing this they can raise the standard of the judiciary to a great height. Hence, like the high officials of the executive, if their term of office is fixed, they find it difficult to work independently. In this respect, the US federal system presents an ideal model, because there the judges of the federal Supreme Court are in office for an indefinite period, provided they are physically fit. In India, however, this practice is not in 'vogue'. Here, of course the term of office of the judges of higher courts is a little longer than that of the high officials of government. For instance, the retiring age of the judges of the high courts is 62 years and that of the judges of the Supreme Court is 65 years. This, however, is not determined by a law made by the legislature which would have surely affected the independence of the judiciary. To ensure this independence, the Indian Constitution fixes the retiring age of the judges of the Supreme Court and High Courts.

Third, independence of the judiciary also depends on the stability and security of service of the judges. Indeed, they can hardly work independently if in this matter they have to depend on others. Thus, if the executive, which is empowered to appoint the judges, may at will remove them, the latter may always fear the diktat of the executive authority. If so, they cannot work independently and impartially. Hence, there should be a rule that they may be removed from office only on grounds of proved incapacity or misbehaviour and that may be done only by following a difficult process. Britain and India follow this rule. In these countries, the constitutional rule is that the judges of higher courts may be removed by the executive only when charges against them on grounds of proved misbehaviour or incapacity are supported by two-thirds majority of both the houses of Parliament. Again, impartiality and independence of the judiciary are harmed if the emolument and allowances of the judges are reduced during their term and if the expenses on that account are subject to legislative approval. This is why the Indian Constitution has laid down that the salary and allowances of Supreme Court and High Court judges shall not be reduced during their term of office and that the money spent for this shall be charged on the consolidated fund, that is, shall not be subject to legislative approval.

Fourth, efficiency of a high standard of the judges is also an important condition for independence of the judiciary. The judiciary indeed will be able to assert its independent authority when the judges are well-versed in the law and the constitution. So, in almost all democratic countries, judges are appointed on the basis of their worth and experience. Only the US system is an exception to this as here political considerations get priority in the appointment of judges.

Last, autonomy of the judicial organ of government is a primary requisite for independence of the judiciary. If the judiciary is not allowed to function independently of the other two organs of government, under the influence of the latter it may lose its independence. Besides, it cannot do its task of protecting the freedom and rights of the individual against the State impartially. So it is essential to keep the judiciary completely separate from the other two organs of government. It may be mentioned that in India, under Article 50 of the Constitution, judiciary has been completely separated from the executive.

16

CHAPTER

Social and Political Changes

Notes

INTRODUCTION

The world never stands still. It is in continuous flux. No wonder the history of mankind is a history of change, particularly social and political change. In early times, man watching changes around took them as preordained. So he took them as spontaneously happening in which he had no role to play. In the mediaeval period, tutored in the teachings of Church of Rome, he was convinced that everything was due to divine grace and accordingly he felt that he was just a passive spectator and never an actor of changes. The 15th-century European Renaissance, however, forced a radical change in this stagnant belief and attitude. Rediscovering anew his self, man now realized that he could be an effective agent of changes. This realization was put into practice by Martin Luther who in the early 16th century initiated the Reformation movement which brought to pieces the erstwhile religious beliefs, thereby proving that man is capable of forcing changes. The Reformation movement was followed successively by the Puritan Revolution beginning in 1640, the Glorious Revolution of 1688, the French Revolution of 1789, the 18th-century Age of Enlightenment and the Industrial Revolution of the 18th–19th century. All these were ample pieces of evidence of human capability of ushering in changes in society and politics. Indeed, whenever Karl Marx in the 19th century observed that philosophers have so far interpreted the world, but the point however is to change it, he actually underscored the confidence that man alone is the maker of history and the architect of social and political changes.

Notes

Thus, in the modern world, it is universally agreed that change is possible and only by conscious human effort. In fact, modernity is the other name of change, for modernity presupposes dynamism and looking forward, and hence constant changes. True, in every modern society, there is a conservative section that, clung to the past, refuses to welcome changes. To them, whatever is modern by way of changes in the life of man is much worse than what was in the 'golden' past. But modernity does not care for them. It advances forward, bringing in continuously quantitative and qualitative changes. The quality of change, however, depends on the intention of those who work for it. If the intention is good, that is, if it is committed to true public interest, it brings in a better state of things. On the other hand, if the urge for change is led by selfish private interest, it causes disaster to the people. Mussolini and Hitler, of course, were keen on inviting changes. But as their will to change was incited by a wild urge to establish firmly their one-man authority, it finally ruined them and their regime and permanently marked them as disgraced heroes of history. On the contrary, Gandhi continued a long and peaceful struggle for change in India dedicated to the cause of humanity. Hence, he is still respectfully remembered by the world.

IMPORTANCE OF CHANGE

Of social and political change, which one is more important is a question that has been chasing theorists for long. There are some who are led by the conviction that politics is the main factor behind social change. That is, according to them, the State is the leading actor in effecting social changes. On the other hand, there are others who believe that society is the determinant of political change. According to them, political change depends on the social base. Unless the society is aptly fit for political change, all attempts on the part of the State to bring social change must end in failure. Needless to say, the first view is held by those who are advocates of democracy. Since they have immense faith on the workability of a democratic State, they naturally argue that a democratic State is the most efficient agent of social change. The second view is that of the Marxists. As they view the society characterized by modes of production serving as the base and the State with all its institutions as the superstructure, and as they believe that the base conditions the superstructure, they are of firm belief that social change determines the political change.

As the recent happenings in the world have proved the utter inapplicability of Marxism and as democracy is continuing its triumphant march, the second view noted above proves now as rather incorrect. Thus, the first view appears to be winning over the second. Yet the second view must not be altogether dismissed. Actually, the best and most reasonable way to resolve the conundrum is to integrate the first view with the second view, and this indeed may be done in the following manner.

Notes

If the society is not ready for change, despite the best efforts of the State, social change is not possible. That is, if the society, because of its nature, cannot overwhelmingly accept a basic change in its order, all attempts by the State to bring in this change are likely to end in failure. For instance, though as a result of reasoned and sustained movement by Ishwar Chandra Vidyasagar, a celebrated social reformer of the 19th-century Bengal, Lord Dalhousie, the then Governor General of India, in 1856 enacted a law in favour of widow marriage, it fell through because the then prevailing feudal society found it incongruent with its culture. Again, after India had become a sovereign State with parliamentary democracy as its system of government, Jawaharlal Nehru rightly felt that this kind of modern government would hardly fit in with the then predominantly rural society of India governed by feudal values. This is why as the first prime minister of India he gave much emphasis on the development of urban society by way of rapid industrialization. These are the instances of how social change may be a determinant of political change. Further, sometimes it may so happen that under the influence of democratic political institutions and by virtue of regular political participation in the democratic process, people living in a society abjure their old beliefs and traditional customs and make themselves sufficiently modern to embrace a social change. This exemplifies how the State may be a dependable actor of social change, that is, how politics serves as an agent of social change. Thus, it is futile to dispute about the validity of one or other of the views noted above. Actually, in a sense both the views are correct even when the Marxist stand is discarded.

Marx in his dialectical materialism was right in postulating that change is natural and inevitable. However, he never meant to say that this change automatically takes place. This is indeed very true of social change. It is by no means a self-generated spontaneous process. Someone must take the initiative to set it in motion. Sometimes this initiative is taken by political leadership but not necessarily, as at some other times social leadership may take an active role in this matter. For instance, in India Vinoba Bhave, a noted social leader, began a social movement known as Bhoodan Movement by which he asked the affluent landowners to make a gift of a part of their lands to the landless. Again, Sunderlal Bahuguna gave leadership in launching a historic movement known as Chipko movement in which women in groups embraced trees in order to prevent them from being cut down by the contractors employed by money-hunting businessmen. This movement finally gave birth to a new society conscious of the urgent need for conservation of forestry in India. Further, Gandhi's sustained campaign against untouchability, a legacy of mediaeval feudal society, attained significant success as it made most of the Indian people averse to this evil practice. Remembering that Gandhi was not just a political leader but also a social leader, it may be said that Indian history provides a strong evidence that social leadership may be an effective actor of social change. Thus, both political leadership and social leadership may serve as an agent of social change.

Notes

As regards political change, society no doubt often influences it. After all, political change is essentially a consequential response to the pressing needs and demands of society. Thus, in Europe it was only after the Renaissance had fundamentally changed the social scenario that traditional political set-up began undergoing basic changes. Again, when by the middle of the 19th century English Industrial Revolution laid bare the untold sufferings of the working class, the English state which was confined to the shell of its individualist non-interference was nowcompelled to turn into an interventionist State, which later led T. H. Green to give a collectivist dimension to liberalism. However, the fact remains that power is the final and formal architect of political change. Social demands reach them through a well-organized communicative process and after considering the pros and cons of such demands they take decisions and implement them.

MODE OF CHANGE

What then is the mode of social and political change? It is a question one may hardly avoid while discussing changes in society and politics. The social movement for social change is generally peaceful and non-violent. In England, Bertrand Russell, a noted philosopher, launched a social movement in the early 1960s in order to press the government to go in for unilateral nuclear disarmament. But to do this, he organized peaceful sit-in demonstrations, public meetings, campaigns and so on. In the early 21st century, Anna Hazare in India continued peaceful assemblage demonstrations and so on to force the government to create the institution of Lokpal (Indian substitute of Ombudsman). In March 2018, 30,000 peasants marched on foot from Nasik to Mumbai in order to put in their demands without causing any disturbance to anyone. If however, the social movement for social change turns violent, it no longer remains purely a social movement, for it is often found that political parties to serve their electoral interest stand by the social movement and incite violence, and thus the social movement takes the form of a political movement. This is found to be commonplace in India.

The political authority, and nobody else, is empowered to make political changes. But those seated in political power always desperately try to maintain status quo ruling out any necessity of political change, as they know well that any political change might dislodge them from the seat of power or at least make things inconvenient or uncomfortable for them. This is why the mode is extremely important in matters of political change. Actually, it is only a strong political movement that may force a political change. Whenever the State miserably fails to ensure equitable distribution of resources and encourages concentration of wealth, a large section of people suffers from an acute sense of deprivation and frustration, and naturally they begin longing for a new political system that would put an end to their tragedy. This is what incites a political

Notes

movement for change. This political movement is generally a protest movement. Thus, a protest may rightfully be regarded as a mode of political change.

Everywhere a protest is usually found to be peaceful in so far as it takes the form of verbal or written criticism by an individual or a group, mass petitions, peaceful picketing, demonstration, public meetings and marches, and, as often used by Gandhi in India, fast, non-violent civil disobedience and non-cooperation. All this may be for political reform or what Popper calls 'piecemeal change'. But whenever the demand for reform or piecemeal change, raised by the protest movement, goes unheeded and consequently the patience of those who lead this movement reaches a breaking point, the peaceful movement assumes a violent form. That is, the resistance envisaged by the protest movement turns into a violent revolution. Karl Marx, who consistently held the view that change is always a violent change resulting from the intensity of contradiction between the forces of production and the relations of production, naturally propounded a full-length theory of revolution, later supplemented by Lenin. But as in actual practice Marx's theory of revolution has failed to produce the results it assured, revolution has rather been outdated in modern times. Further, democracy by nature is averse to violent revolution, as it is taken for granted in this system that some kind of political change is quite possible by virtue of periodic elections which are a means for freely expressing people's political choice. And as in the 21st century democracy seems to have got almost a walkover, Marxian revolution is now regarded just as a theoretical exercise with hardly any feasibility.

However, besides Marxian revolution, there may be another kind of revolution taking place even in democracies. Although strictly speaking it is actually a pseudo revolution, it no doubt denotes radical change as it replaces the very democratic system. This kind of revolution takes place whenever the army with an extreme lust for power and political ambition wrests power by force from the democratic rulers and replaces a democratic government by an arbitrarily ruling despotic government. The people fed on democratic values cannot resist this political change as they are forced to acquiesce in this drastic political change that absolutely denies people's freedom. Although this kind of political change is not a change for the better but the worse, it is admittedly a revolution as it signifies a complete change of the prevailing political system. This has been witnessed in a good many countries of Latin America and of a number of Afro-Asian States, including Pakistan and even Bangladesh in the past.

The army quitting its barrack is able to be crowned with political power because it has certain characteristics that completely differentiate it from other groups active in the political system. First, by virtue of its activities, it is much more organized than any other civilian organization. Second, it has a highly centralized command and a hierarchical structure marked by unwavering discipline. After all, the basic objective of the army is to fight as a single unit to defend the country against any war or foreign aggression. This explains why the military command is very much centralized. Third, for the same reason the army is arranged in a hierarchal order, for the centralized command easily transmits its orders from the highest to the lowest level, and therefore every lower rank is mentally oriented to carry out the orders of the immediately higher rank. Fourth, the army works under strict discipline. Indeed, every soldier is tutored to regard himself as a depersonalized part of a machine, who does not question the inviolability of the established chain of commands and is mentally ready to strictly obey the rules. Fifth, the army always has in its possession a very elaborate and effective system of intercommunication, as a result of which it is marked by a unity of decision and action notwithstanding the fact that its various units are spread over a country. Sixth, the army everywhere is kept completely separated from the civilian society by various means such as separate barracks, distinctive uniforms and the indoctrination of the new recruits in the history and tradition of the army. This generates among the members of the armed forces a military culture naturally not shared by members of the civilian society. Last, the army enjoys a near monopoly over the instruments of force and violence.

Notes

It would be wrong to suggest that these characteristics by themselves stir up the army to politically intervene. These are only the indices to demonstrate their ability to be politically overactive. However, the ability of the army hardly makes room for its political intervention. Actually, the army makes intervention in the political process only when opportunities on that score are available to it. These opportunities depend on several objective conditions. For instance, first, when a democratic country is at war, the civilian authority may be too much dependent on the army as the former has little knowledge about the technicalities. Even after the war or the war-like situation is over, this dependence may continue and this may make the army overpowerful, which eventually may make it hungry for political power. Second, a domestic crisis may also increase the influence of the army on the civilian ruler, as confronted with a serious domestic crisis which the standing police force is unable to cope with, a government may take the help of the army and thereby may make itself more dependent on the army. Third, the army having had a spectacular victory in war may enjoy great popularity or prestige and thus may turn itself into a potential threat to the civilian rule. Fourth, and the most important one, is utter inefficiency of the government clearly evident to the people. This inefficiency may be due to corruption of the government, political intrigue, criminalization of politics and so on, which may shatter the confidence of the people in the existing civilian government, and this may facilitate military intervention in the politics of the country. In fact, as history shows, most of the military interventions in the world have been due to mismanagement in governance, utter failure of the government in delivering goods to the people and also its involvement in wide corrupt practices. Thus, precisely the army turns to political power when effective political institutions are absent, power is fragmented and, as a result, the entire society goes out of gear. However,

Notes

if the civil society is extremely strong, keeps a constant vigil over the lapses of the government and creates a strong public opinion in favour of spontaneous resistance against the failures of the government, chances are that the latter will mend its lapses and put back governance in order. In Pakistan, it may be noted that it is because of the absence of a powerful civil society that the army has been able to intervene again and again or has virtually controlled the political decision-makers without trying a formal takeover of government.

However, it is the teaching of modern political history that revolutionary political change by way of military intervention has never been able to ensure a stable and long-lived political authority, for the military masters, with little political knowledge and experience, are naturally incapable of efficiently combating the social and political problems that paved the way for their despotic rule. Maybe initially by effecting some quick and dramatic changes they may attain a little success in cleaning the Augean stable, but in the long run they fail to efficiently deliver goods to the people. Hence, the recent history of military rule has been a history of the failure of the men in barrack to achieve political legitimacy. Again, drastic curtailment of political freedom of people under the army rule they enjoyed long in a democratic state generates dissatisfaction among them. At a certain stage when this army rule gets involved in corruption without caring for public sentiments, the growing dissatisfaction of the people may suddenly explode into a strong mass movement challenging the authority of the men 'on the horseback' and threatening their seat of power. Hence, the radical political change by way of military intervention is no real solution to the social and political problems confronting a country. That indeed is the verdict of history.

17

CHAPTER

Crisis of Indian Political Theory

INTRODUCTION

Notes

As the Afro-Asian nations with colonial heritage were for long under the dependency of the Western political rulers, even after they emerged as independent nations, they have been unable to renounce the colonial legacy. This is why in many of the sectors of their national life such as lingua franca, lifestyle, national development and politics, they are still found to be under Western influence. No wonder in the theory of politics taught in the academic institutions of these countries, one notices a predominant influence of Western political theories and a tragic failure to evolve an indigenous political theory in conformity with their own characteristic social and political conditions which are completely different from the Western historical conditions. Thus, political theory, as read and studied in the academic circles of these countries, is yet to achieve independence. Independent India is naturally no exception in this regard.

In the 20th century, until India became independent in 1947, those who dealt with or dwelt on political theory were all under the influence of the Western model. They readily accepted the credibility and feasibility of Western political ideas and concepts, and in their writings and discourses followed them faithfully. The only exceptions among them were M. K. Gandhi and Professor Benoy Kumar Sarkar, a noted social scientist of Bengal, working as a teacher of political science in the University of Calcutta. In his *Hind Swaraj*, Gandhi

Notes

presented a theory of politics which did not have an iota of Western influence and therefore was highly original. At a time when most of the Western political theorists were employing arguments to justify the sovereign authority of the State and some among them seemed euphoric about the sterling merit of a parliamentary democratic system, Gandhi rejected both on the respective grounds that the State is inimical to individual freedom and an embodiment of force and violence, and that the parliamentary system surrenders to unwholesome party interests. On the basis of this rejection, Gandhi developed his own theory of politics. He felt that the best way to ensure individual freedom was complete decentralization of power. Accordingly, he took his envisioned gram swaraj as the best substitute of the state system. He envisaged that every self-sufficient village would be the basic unit of the political system in which every villager, with his participation in decision-making and responsibility to save his village from external attack, would enjoy power along with others equally. This, no doubt, is a novel system. But unfortunately, in modern conditions, it is not workable. However, it does not bear any Western influence.

In the four volumes of *The Positive Background of Hindu Sociology*, which was his magnum opus, Benoy Kumar Sarkar with meticulous logic and enough historical pieces of evidence discarded the spiritual heritage of India, as underscored by Max Müller and other Western writers, and established his central thesis that India has all along been following a secular tradition. This led him to develop a secular view of life. Naturally, unlike the contemporary Indian theorists who devotedly were following the Western idealist view of the State and were much under the influence of T. H. Green, an English idealist political philosopher of the 19th century, he developed a secular view of the State. Thus, Sarkar was the first Indian political theorist in dependent India to provide a secular foundation of the State.

It was in this context that Sarkar expounded a theory of the State which he styled as 'realistic'. In this theory, Sarkar dismissed the idea of the State as a mystic entity. To him, the State is as much human and temporal as any other modern association and institution. Second, according to him the State is not an eternal institution at work since time immemorial. At a certain historical stage, there was society but no State and there might be a similar situation in future. Thus, the State is always different from society and its distinctive feature that differentiates it from society is that it is invariably marked by a mechanism known as government. Third, the State is not a natural institution that has spontaneously evolved. It actually is an artificial institution, a deliberate creation of man. It indeed comes into being whenever people voluntarily agree to form it. Fourth, the State is essentially an elite State. That is, the idea that it is run by many, that is, the people is just a myth. It is actually run by one or a few or, to say more clearly, by a few business tycoons. Thus, everywhere the State is run by a wealthy few; that is, the State is always a plutocratic State. Fifth, taking cue

Notes

from Aristotle, some Western political theorists tried to justify the coercive authority of the State on moral considerations. But Benoy Kumar Sarkar unhesitatingly identified the State as an embodiment of force. According to him, this force is necessary for the State to effectively deal with internal disturbance as well as to defend itself from external aggression. Last, according to Sarkar, though the State emerges out of the will of the people to form it by way of a voluntary agreement among them to bring it into existence, it is also a product of interaction of various national and international factors. That is, the birth of a State depends not only on the subjective will of the people but also on objective conditions. This indeed reflects his pragmatic approach to the question of the State.

But what kind of government would be the best type for a State? To give an answer to this question, Benoy Kumar Sarkar introduced a novel concept which he styled as 'demo-despotocracy'. It is a form of government that represents a mixture of democracy and despotism. He was aware of the contemporary theoretical stand that despotism is opposed to democracy. Yet he held the view that despotism is really complementary to democracy. Actually, he regarded both Hobbes and Rousseau as right in that, in his opinion, it was an undisputable reality that the State cannot work without extreme physical force. But then the State, as an embodiment of coercion, must earn legitimacy from the people and this is possible only when people voluntarily consent to obey this coercive State. This is why he recommended a form of government that would integrate both the despotic and democratic elements. Perhaps he suggested this integration for two reasons. First, he had a close link with the regimes of Mussolini and Hitler and, accordingly, was attracted by the disciplined order of these two regimes. At the same time, he was convinced of the merits of the democratic system. Second, he felt that when his country would be free from foreign rule, India's traditional society would hardly be able to fully digest democracy. But the fact is that Sarkar's 'demo-despotocracy' is an impossible idea to realize and so it was strongly criticized by his contemporaries. The progressive Indian political actors of his time even went to the extent of ostracizing him as a fascist agent. It is true that Benoy Kumar Sarkar's theory of politics seems to be based on pure conviction, unsupported by cogent and well-organized arguments. Yet it would be unkind not to recognize his genius. After all, he was an Indian theorist who presented a highly original theory in dependent India.

POST-INDEPENDENCE SITUATION

After India achieved independence, Indian political theory started its journey without any direction. Indeed, starved of ideas it seemed to be suffering from confusion and bewilderment. Actually, the Western political ideas of the pre-Second World War period dominated the thinking of Indian political theorists at that time. Meanwhile, in the 1950s and 1960s the American political science

Notes

stirred the theoretical world of politics by offering some ideas without any precedent. For instance, they deserted the idea of the State. Second, in their urge to make the study of politics purely empirical, they sounded a farewell to philosophy which for hundreds of years had served as a guide to political theory. Against this backdrop were produced various theoretical models on politics such as behaviouralism, systems analysis, communications model and structural–functional analysis. The moment these new ideas reached Indian political theorists, they enthusiastically welcomed them taking them as the only way to modernize Indian political theory. Thus, Indian political theory so long groping in the dark for a direction seemed to have got it like a sinking boat finding at last a rescue team to take it to safety. Indeed, among the Indian political theorists, there was a great euphoria about the American value-free and empirical political theory which much influenced them. Naturally, in the study, teaching and research conducted by Indian political scientists, empirical political theory and approach received the highest priority. However, when in the late 1980s American empirical political science began losing its edge and turned back to philosophy as its primary base at the insistence of some of the noted political theorists of the USA, the table was turned and there set in a trend to focus the importance of value-oriented politics.

At this juncture, the crisis of Indian political theory loomed large—a crisis that has been still continuing. The Indian political theorists, of course, eventually abjured to a large extent the empirical tradition, but they did not know how best to integrate philosophy and consequently values with politics, despite the fact that India is a country with a long philosophical tradition in its intellectual history. Further, the old habit of Indian political theorists to accept without question what comes through the Western window always dies hard. As a result, none of the Indian political theorists has ever tried to develop an Indian political theory suited to India's objective conditions. It may be noted that the wise men in the Indian Constituent Assembly framed a constitution deriving elements from different Western constitutions without trying to draw up the fundamental law of the land at parity with the specificities of Indian conditions. All this has led to a disaster in that a wide gap between theory and practice of politics is frequently found in India, a phenomenon almost unknown in Western countries. Further, Indian political theory patently unable to infuse values in politics appears to be completely irrelevant to the practice of politics in India.

This then is the crisis of present-day Indian political theory. The crisis, it may be added, is encouraging today the rampant use of so-called political intrigues and corruption among Indian political actors. To resolve this growing crisis, Indian political theorists have surely an important role to play. For instance, first they should try to evolve a purely Indian political theory, taking a careful account of Indian conditions that may bridge the gap between theory and practice of

Notes

politics in India. Second, they should bear in mind that the task of a political theorist is not only to have a well-thought-out idea but also to give directions to the indigenous political process. Last, in order to counter the tendency of the political actors to indulge in evil and immoral practices, they have to fix a moral goal of political theory much after the Western political philosophers such as Aristotle, T. H. Green and others. They may, thus, evolve morals of politics badly required by modern Indian politics. Briefly, by all this, they may be able to cure Indian politics of all evils.

Index

Age of Enlightenment and the Industrial Revolution of 18th–19th century, 156
anarchism, 113, 118, 118–122
  English Industrial Revolution, 118
  William Godwin, 118

bureaucracy, 148–150

cabinet dictatorship, 142
chief executive 146–148
citizen, 86
  characteristics, 88–89
  duties and rights, 89–90
citizenship, 87
  new dimensions, 91–92
  involvement of Romans, 87
civil society, 28
  democracy, 33–34
    fundamentalism, 34
    government policies, 34
    lapses, detection, 34
    media role, 35
    strength and viability, touchstone, 34
  Gramsci's theory, 30
  India, 32–33
  liberal view, 29
    liberal political system, 33
    social leadership, 33
  Locke, 29
  Marxist view, 29
  nature, 30
    liberal framework, 31
    responsibility, 32
    viability and success, 31

delegated legislation, 143
demo-despotocracy, 165
democracy, 102
  consociational, 108–110
  critiques, 110–111
  developmental, 107–108
  form of government, 103–105
  participatory, 108
  Third World, 105–106
democratic political systems, 58

economic equality
  Marxist theory, 58
economic liberalism, 116
English Industrial Revolution, 118
Enquiry Concerning Political Justice, 118
equality, 55–62
  Harold Laski, view, 56
  man's sense, 55
  Marxist theory, failure, 57
  types, 57
    democratic political systems, 58
    economic equality, 58
    legal equality, 58
    religious equality, 57–58
    social equality, 58
executive, 144–148

fascism, 113, 127–130
fascist corporate State
  characteristics, 129
freedom, 54
  community, 47
  community leader, 47
  evolution of concept, 48–49
  human civilization, paradoxes, 47
  non-slave owning class, 48
  possibility, 53
    subjective freedom, 53
    traditional agriculture-oriented societies, 53
  social control, 47

Gandhism, 113, 131–137
  Brahmacharya, 132
  non-violence, 132
  religion, 131
  sarvodaya, 134
  state 135–136
  satyagraha, 134–135
  swaraj, 133–134
globalization, 91
government, 20–22, 138 –155
  presidential and parliamentary form, 140
  theory of separation of powers, 138

Hind Swaraj, 135, 163
human rights
  UN Declaration, 68

ideology
  Karl Marx's view, 112
Indian political theory
  crisis, 163–167
    demo-despotocracy, 165
    theory of Sarkar, 164 –165
individual freedom, 51–52
inequality in society, 56

judiciary, 150–155
justice, 71–79
  nature, 78–79
  Rawls' theory, 75–77
  theoretical concept, 71

law, 80–85
  Austin's theory, 81
  Baker's view, 82–83
  Harold Laski's view, 82
  Henry Maine's theory, 82
  indubitable means, 81
  moral purpose, 81
  nature, 84–85
  State, 83–84
legal equality, 58
legal justice, 72
legislature, 139–144
  Bagehot, view, 140–141
  decline, 142–143
  functions, 140–142
  importance, 143
  Indian Constitution, 139
  judicial powers, 141
  laws, 141
  liberal democratic system, 139
  modern democracy, 143
  The English Constitution, 140
  upper house, 139
liberalism, 113–118
  economic, 116
  pluralist, 116
Libertarianism, 116–117

Manual of Political Economy, 116
Marxism, 113, 122–127
  source, 122
Marxist theory of economic equality, 58
modern theory of politics, 71
moral conscience, 10

parliamentary democracy, 140
pluralist liberalism, 116
political freedom, 50–51
political ideology, 112–137
  anarchism, 113, 118–122
  fascism, 113, 127–130
  Gandhism, 113, 131–137
  liberalism, 113, 113–118
  Marxism, 113, 122–127
political justice, 72
political power, 37
political science
  theory and thought, 3–5
politics, 1
  study, 5–7
Positive Background of Hindu Sociology, 164
power, 36–45
  authority, 43–45
    legitimacy, 43
    Max Weber's classification, 43–45
    power holder, 43

tradition, 43
compliance, 40–41
forms, 38
persuasion, 37
politics, 39
sources, 37
Chinese socialist system, 42
democracy ideology, 42
issues, 42
Talcott Parsons, 42
primary goods, 76

Rawls' theory of justice, 75–77
realistic
theory of State by Sarkar, 164
religious equality, 57–58
rights, 63–70
Advisory Committee of the Constituent Assembly of India, 68
individual, 68
man, 69–70
meaningful use, 66–67
revolution, 69
source, 64–66
theoretical level, 64
social and political changes, 156–162
importance, 157–159
social equality, 58–59
the case of India, 59–62
social justice, 72
Renaissance and after, 74–75
pre-Renaissance conceptualization, 72–74
social power, 36–37
social right, 68
society, 8–14
evolution, 10–11
sociology, 28
sovereignty, 20–22
State and society, 11–14
liberal State, 12
modern history, 11
secularism, 12
State, 15–27
law, 0–5
obedience, 22–25
parliamentary system, 17
Platonic reality, 17
qualities, 16
related riddles, ideas, 18–19
roll back, 15
sovereignty, 20–22

The English Constitution, 140
The General Idea of the Revolution in the Nineteenth Century, 119
The Political System, 2
theory of separation of powers, 138

UN Declaration of Human Rights, 68
US federal Supreme Court, 18